The Marshall Chronicles

Aim High

Capturing Moments
in a
Military Chaplain's Journey

Randy Marshall

AIM HIGH: Capturing Moments in a military chaplain's journey

© Copyright 2024 M Randy Marshall
ISBN: 978-1-962848-09-1

Interior and cover design: Marji Laine

 Published by:
Roaring Lambs Publishing
17110 Dallas Parkway, Suite 260
Dallas, TX 75248

Published in the United States of America.

Dedication

This book is dedicated
to my family
and the men and women
who serve our nation
through the Armed Forces.

Contents

Preface

"It always seems impossible until it's done"
Nelson Mandela

I remember it well.

1985—Southwestern Baptist Theological Seminary

Conversation with a classmate outside a Pastoral Ministry class.

The conversation culminated with these words: "You want to be an Air Force chaplain? You might as well kiss that goodbye!"

This classmate wasn't attacking my ministerial, intellectual, or physical abilities. In fact, I hardly even knew him. He had simply heard that I was exploring the possibility of becoming an Air Force Reserve chaplain. In his "immense knowledge" of the military, he knew that at this point in our nation's history, it was extremely difficult to enter the Air Force, even through the Reserve Forces.

He didn't stop there. He continued, "If you want to join the military, you need to join the Army." In my brashness I answered, "I don't know if the Lord is calling me into the Air Force, but I know He wouldn't call me into the Army!" My apologies to my Army friends, but I bled Air Force blue. My father had spent twenty years of Active Duty in the Air Force as an enlisted member working on various aircraft. During the first thirteen years of my life, as a dependent of a military member, I was what some affectionately dub an "Air Force brat." During those early years, our family—dad, mom, and older sister, lived on Air Force bases in

Alaska, throughout the Continental United States, and Japan. My dad retired when I was in seventh grade near San Antonio, TX. With my background in growing up on Air Force bases and my perceived differences in culture between the Army and the Air Force, I was led to an Air Force path, even if the path seemed unlikely or even impossible.

It always seems impossible until it's done.

It was not the first time that I faced impossible. When I felt the call to ministry, I was sixteen years old. My early attempts at leading Bible Studies and preaching were unimpressive. I didn't stand out in a crowd. One of my High School English teachers who attended the church I attended, took me aside one day after class and asked, "Are you sure God has called you to preach?" Ouch! In the summer after my High School Graduation, I had a casual conversation with one of my adult neighbors and told her I was headed to college. She replied in a very surprised and deliberate tone, "You're going to college?" So, yes, I went to college and yes, I graduated and continued my theological education.

It always seems impossible until it's done.

Back to my Seminary conversation, the reason I had an interest in the military chaplaincy was due in large part to a professor who was serving in the Air Force Reserve as a chaplain. He would tell stories of unique and exciting experiences and how the Lord was able to use him to speak into the lives of Airmen and their families. It was a light-bulb moment when I realized I could be a local church pastor and an Air Force Reserve chaplain as well. Despite the odds of ever being able to join the Air Force, I pressed forward with the denominational application to obtain an ecclesiastical endorsement—a necessary step to serving as a military chaplain. Honestly, after that, I forgot about it.

Three years later, I received a call from a denominational representative informing me that, if I still desired, a slot had opened and, I was offered the opportunity to join. I accepted the offer. So, at the ripe age of twenty-nine, I received a commission as a First Lieutenant in the United States Air Force Reserve to serve as a chaplain. It was a decision I have never regretted. It became a 30-year career in both part-time and full-time military service culminating in my last position as Command Chaplain of the Air Force Reserve Command. By God's grace, hard work, understanding churches, and a loving family, I was able to complete the course set before me.

It always seems impossible until it's done.

"The Marshall Chronicles: Aim High" takes a look back at my experiences as a Reserve Air Force chaplain from 1989–2008 and full-time service from 2008-2020. The account is certainly not exhaustive, rather it contains memories that have stuck with me over the years. Though the story is wrapped in a military setting with some military vernacular, I have attempted to tell the story in a conversational manner that appeals to a large audience. For those interested, I have also added a section toward the end of the book entitled, "Flight Notes" that gives an even deeper explanation of particular topics. In addition, throughout this book, I have attempted to spell out all acronyms. As a help to the reader, an alphabetical list of acronyms and descriptions are included after the "Flight Notes" section.

The purpose of this book is three-fold. First, no matter who you are, what you do, or where you live, God is continually present and active. Hopefully, through this account, you can be aware or reminded that God can mold and shape the improbable or even the impossible aspects of your lives. Secondly, I hope you enjoy this behind-the-scenes look at one Air Force military chaplain. Let me emphasize, this is my story. Every chaplain will have a different perspective. Every chaplain has a unique set of experiences. Third, whether you have a military background or not, I hope you can appreciate both the serious and humorous sides of the life of a military chaplain.

Introduction

Years ago, I had a doctor's appointment. It was one of those appointments where I had to strip down and don a terry-cloth wrap. So, I felt particularly vulnerable. The doctor came in, looked at my medical chart where it noted my occupation: "chaplain." Without looking up he asked, "So what is the difference between a chaplain, a minister, a rabbi, and a priest?" He looked at me, I looked at him, both of us sensed an uncomfortable silence. Finally, I blurted out, "Oh, I'm sorry, I thought you were telling me a joke!"

We both laughed. It reminded me that there can be some confusion, even among the most educated, about the role of a chaplain. Chaplains can be found in a variety of settings—military environments, police departments, fire departments, businesses, hospitals, sport teams, and various other institutions. Chaplains can serve in both part-time and full-time capacities. Chaplains represent a variety of religious backgrounds—Christian primarily, but also Jewish, Muslim, and Buddhist, to name a few. The hallmark of chaplains is the closeness to the community they serve. The most effective chaplains are intertwined with the institutional setting. They know the unique acronyms, the stressors, and the overall culture. Unlike a local church minister who may occasionally visit someone in these environments, chaplains are on staff and part of the team. In my civilian experience as a pastor, I would have been welcome to visit the businesses where my congregation worked. I would have been welcome to visit and even speak to the local high school or college sports teams. I would have been welcomed, and they would have politely shown me around, but they would not have seen me as part of their culture and setting. I would have been an outsider coming into their world and then leaving. A chaplain presence is different. He or she brings a particular skill set that is intertwined in the overall culture and work of the institution. All chaplains receive specialized training and experience in these settings.

On the surface, the effectiveness of the chaplain may be questioned. What value does a minister bring to the institution? What kind of difference do they make? Insightful leaders see the presence of the chaplain as invaluable. In the hospital, the chaplain is available to listen, encourage, and pray for patients and hospital staff. For First Responders and the military, having a chaplain available during intense times of grief and stress can bring restoration and renewed strength. Not only are the physical and mental needs addressed, but oftentimes spiritual. The individuals he/she ministers may or may not have a faith background, but spiritual matters always seem to rise to the surface. Some of the most intense and meaningful spiritual conversations I have experienced have been in a hospital room, in a funeral home, on a flight line, and moments where a member takes me aside and says, "chaplain, I need to talk with you." Though the concept of a chaplain, with multiple religious views represented may appear to be quaint and the beginning of a punch line, the impact of an effective chaplain is no joke! Powerful, life-changing, transformations can take place. It is no joke, but as you will see, at times it can be a bit funny!

As I noted in my previous book of this trilogy, "The Marshall

Chronicles: Farm-to-Market Edition," for twenty-two years, I pastored three Texas churches. In nineteen of those years, I also served as a Reserve Air Force chaplain. In 2008, I transitioned from serving as Pastor of the First Baptist Church, Dickinson, TX to a full-time military chaplain position in Miami, FL. Vocationally this was a risky move. U.S. Congress limits the number of days a full-time reservist can serve in a certain time period under certain types of military orders. I was only given three years as a guarantee. Not only was there uncertainty, there was also a massive personal and vocational transition in the move. My identity as a senior pastor would change to being a staff officer. My wife Susie and I would move from small-town Texas to the hustle and bustle of South Florida. Our living conditions would change from our comfortable four-bedroom home in a suburban neighborhood to an apartment— something we hadn't done since Seminary. With Blake, our son now living in Colorado; Amanda, our daughter, remaining in Dickinson; my sister, Sandy, living in Houston along with my ailing mother; and 100 percent of remaining family and friends being left behind, the decision to move was extremely difficult. Though the transition was hard, I sensed the leading of the Holy Spirit to pack our bags and make the move.

The story begins in 2008 with a drive from Dickinson, TX to Miami FL. With the drive comes a flood of memories.

The Road to Miami

2008

Highway Ponderings

The distance between Dickinson, TX and Miami FL is 1,201 miles. It is a 19-hour drive.

My date to report to the United States Southern Command (USSOUTHCOM) was upcoming. Susie and I decided that I would go ahead to begin working and search for an appropriate place to live. That meant she would stay behind to prepare for the movers and attend to any last-minute details. So, early in the morning, I began a solo drive to Miami in my ten-year old Chevy Malibu. Solo, that is, except for our white and black cat who was not crazy about the trip.

As I headed north on I-45 toward Houston, there was a sense of grief in leaving an area and a church we had spent the last ten years. There was also a sense of relief. Though ministry in Dickinson was extremely gratifying, there was also a shedding of some of the stress that had built up over the years.

Before I was aware of "books on tape (or CD)" and certainly before Podcasts, my mind began to reflect on the past few years and how I got to the point of accepting a full-time military position. As the miles rolled by, so did the memories. With the cat settled comfortably on the back seat, my mind focused on military chaplaincy and my role for the past 20 years. So, my personal "book on tape" began to unfold. Allow me to share some of these rolling, sometimes random thoughts put into a story form illustrated on this drive—the road to Miami

DAY ONE

Forty-five minutes into the nineteen-hour drive

After negotiating the Houston traffic on I-45 north, I began heading due east on I-10 toward Beaumont, Orange, and the Texas border. As the miles rolled by, I began to think about the rich history of military chaplaincy.

Military chaplaincy is not a new idea. It has roots deep in Scripture. It has also been part of the fabric of our nation. The Scripture references priests accompanying troops into battle. Deuteronomy 20:2-4 states, "And it shall be when you are come nigh unto battle that the priest shall approach and speak unto the people." Soldiers in the battlefield were accompanied by spiritual men, priests, who gave the presence of the Holy.

Chaplains will also note a fourth-century legend that provides a picture of mercy and the advent of chaplaincy terms. This story holds that a pagan Roman soldier, Martin of Tours, encountered a beggar shivering from the cold. Martin ripped his military cloak and gave part of it to the man. That night, the soldier had a vision of Jesus dressed in the cloak. Through this encounter, he was immediately drawn and converted to Christianity. Martin of Tours devoted the remainder of his life to the church. After his death, he was canonized and became the patron saint of France. His cloak, now a holy relic, was carried into battle by the Frankish kings. The Latin term for cloak is "cappa." The portable shrine was called the "capella" and its caretaker priest, the "cappellanus."[1] Thus, the chaplain was the keeper of the cloak which was stored in the chapel.

During the mid nineteenth century, England sought western expansion in America, and from 1754-1763, fought in the French and Indian War. During this time, thirty-one chaplains served in the American military. It was during this conflict that a young military officer, George Washington realized the importance and necessity of a military chaplain presence in each unit. For two years, during the war, he tried in vain to persuade Governor Dinwiddle of Virginia to authorize a chaplain for his command, which was then guarding the Virginia frontier. He wrote: "The want of a chaplain does, I humbly conceive, reflect dishonor upon the regiment, as all other officers are allowed. The gentlemen of the corps are sensible to this and did propose to support one at their private expense. But I think it would have a more graceful appearance were he appointed as others are."

When George Washington assumed command of the Continental Army at Cambridge, Massachusetts, he continued to see the importance and impact of the military chaplain. Desperately wanting providence on his side and ensuring his troops to be above reproach, he encouraged the presence of these ministers. He also wanted Soldiers to have a chaplain of their own faith group, so in 1775 he supported the concept of a pluralistic chaplaincy and an Army that would guarantee the free exercise of religion.[2]

This idea was revolutionary in a time when only Anglican clergy could serve as chaplains in the British armies. As religious leaders, they were called upon to visit the wounded, honor the dead, write letters home for soldiers who could not write, and give discourses of a patriotic nature to keep the soldiers from deserting.[3]

Throughout the history of America, chaplains have been intricately weaved into the military culture. For more than 220 years, religion and religious leaders have provided a source of strength and faith for more than 55 million Americans who have served in the military forces of the United States.[4]

In the Air Force, the Chaplain Corps comprises less than half of one percent of personnel. Yet, they are involved in every mission set and available to every Airmen. The Chaplain Corps stands ready to provide spiritual care and ensure all Airmen and their families have opportunities to exercise their Constitutional right to the free exercise of religion.

DAY 1

Two hours into the nineteen-hour drive

Coming to the border of Texas and Louisiana, I reflected on my own, personal journey.

My first part-time Reserve Air Force assignment was at Lackland AFB in San Antonio while serving as pastor of the First Baptist Church in Stockdale, TX. Stockdale is 50 miles Southeast of San Antonio. I served part-time at Lackland from 1989-1999. In the Air Force organization, Lackland is part of the "ATC—the

Air Training Command" which later became "AETC—the Air Education Training Command." Lackland is also dubbed, "The Gateway of the Air Force." For years, Lackland has been the sole basic training base for all enlisted personnel. Young men and women from across the United States, most recent High School graduates, converge on this base where they are immediately thrust into military training. Their hair is cut. For the men, it is shaved. Their sense of identity is shaken.

As they live together, they also learn to work together to build a cohesive unit. This initial military training lasted for six weeks—for the trainees, six long weeks (later the training schedule was expanded.) The days were long and laborious. The pressure to succeed physically and academically was great. Thus, the need, just like in days of the American Revolution, for a chaplain presence was also paramount.

The motivation for young men and women to join the Air Force was varied. Some joined because they felt a strong calling to join the Air Force. Their patriotism was strong. Some joined out of boredom and a lack of direction. Some joined to take advantage of the GI Bill to further their education. Some joined to get away from their girlfriend! These Airmen, with a variety of reasons to join, coming from large metropolitan areas and small towns, from all across the country and the world, were challenged to somehow blend together in a unique military environment. This was the herculean task of the instructors in a six-week timeframe.

Chaplains were assigned and became a part of "Team Lackland"—both Active Duty and Reserve. In the Reserve Air Force Chaplaincy, there are two categories. The first category is the Category (CAT) A, or unit program. Participants in the unit program are known as Traditional Reservists (TR.) In the unit program, military personnel perform their military duty on set, monthly weekends. Reservists may travel long distances to fulfill their training requirements. They normally train two days a month with a two-week annual tour. The personnel are supervised locally by their unit, and all belong to the Air Force Reserve Command. The vast majority of Air Force Reserve personnel are in this category.

Another category of reservists is the Category (CAT) B program, also known as IMAs (Individual Mobilization Augmentees.) The IMA program places reservists in various career fields within Active-Duty bases. Instead of working alongside fellow reservists, IMAs work alongside Active-Duty members. Their purpose is to train with these members and augment the needs of the mission. They are also primarily used as "backfill"—meaning being placed on extended military orders when required. The IMA program is designed to be flexible. Instead of being locked-in to a particular weekend, IMAs can shape their duty into blocks of time, normally during the week. Like the CAT-A members, they also perform a two-week tour at the base, are supervised locally, and are "owned" by the Air Force Reserve Command who monitors all their duty and training. Both programs require approximately 30 days a year. Because of the flexibility for most men and women who are serving in a church or other faith-based institutions, the IMA program has substantially more members in the Chaplain Corps than the CAT-A unit program.

In my 22-year part-time Reserve Duty, I served as an IMA. Lackland AFB was my first encounter with the military as a military member. Everything about it was new. The language, the culture, the rank-structure, relationships, the mission, etc....were worlds apart from my civilian world. I was no longer Bro Randy or Pastor Randy, I was now Chaplain (Ch) Marshall. As a military member, I wore the same military uniform as those I served. Some days I would wear my "blues" (an Air Force uniform—light blue shirt, dark blue pants.) I would also wear what the trainees wore— a Battle Dress Uniform (BDU.) This was a camouflage-patterned uniform that was designed for daily wear. Each of my uniforms had common identifiers including rank, "US Air Force," and "Marshall." An occupational symbol was also on each uniform. My symbol was a cross indicating my job as a chaplain. This badge was both an occupational badge and religious emblem. Over the years the uniforms went through various changes, especially the utility uniform. But these identifiers remained the same.

Duties at Lackland included counseling, visitation (later and more accurately referred to as "religious engagement"), worship, and military briefings. I shudder and smile when I think of the amount of counseling at Lackland. In this pressure-cooker environment, it was important to have someone on base that could be a release valve before they burst. Chaplains were available to serve in this role.

During the week, the chapel foyer became full of sad-faced Airmen who were waiting to see a chaplain. Topics of counseling ranged anywhere from homesickness, physical pain, broken-hearts, mental stress, and the ubiquitous statement, "my recruiter lied to me!" and "I hate the Air Force!" I tried to assure them that this was not the "real" Air Force but was a training environment. I also encouraged them to reflect on why they joined in the first place and what they wanted to accomplish. The best advice I could give is "take it a day at a time", or "even a meal at a time." My silent prayer for most was, "these days of training will pass! God will provide the strength—keep pressing on!"

The counseling session that brings the biggest smile to me was my first. I was brand new. I knew how to counsel but I didn't fully know the military training environment. So, one morning, this big burly teenager in his military uniform, shaved head, and downtrodden countenance came into my office. He towered above me but had the crumpled look of a distressed child. As he sat down, he started talking to me with a volley of military terms and acronyms. I had no clue what they meant. Not wanting to show my ignorance, I simply nodded and showed pastoral support. Then this mountain of a man began to cry—real tears with mucous flowing from his nose. As he wept, he clawed at his bald head and said, "chaplain, I don't want to be here!" I maintained my outward pastoral demeanor. Inside, I was thinking, "Dude, I don't want to be here either!" We both survived that day.

Another important element of the chaplain's day was religious engagement. (Again, this term is preferred over "visitation." As one leader stated, I "visit" my grandmother, I "engage" with my Airmen.) Ask any commander and his/her number one desire for the chaplain is to be with the Airmen. (Note: The term, "commander" means a military superior who is responsible for the conduct of their subordinates. Commanders are found at all levels of the military organization.) Continual Airman engagement was particularly important in this training environment. It was also exceedingly difficult. Since the training was very regulated and prescribed, it was important to be present but not get in the way. Chaplains had to be knowledgeable about what was taking place during the training. What appeared to be confusing and insensitive was actually meeting the training objective to transform these young men and women into military members. Walking into their world– whether in a training environment, in an office, on the flightline, during a field exercise, or any number of places—was a huge privilege and responsibility. No matter who I came in contact, I was "their chaplain." It didn't matter what faith they possessed, if any. I was available for casual conversation or deeper counseling—simply a listening ear to their professional and personal needs.

It was a time of training for me as well. Military chaplains are both ministers and officers. The minister part, I thought I had down, but I still needed to accustom myself to being an officer. Though a First Lieutenant on most bases would not receive a second look, at Lackland, on the Basic Training side of the base, officers, all officers were held in high regard. It is here that I was fortunate to have an Active-Duty chaplain, Captain to mentor me.

This chaplain initially accompanied me on religious engagements to the squadrons. Though I don't know this for sure and never asked, I am sure the Lt Col chaplain who was over the Basic Training, Gateway Chapel took this chaplain aside and said something like, "We have this new Reserve chaplain on our staff.

He is about as green as they come—stick with him so he doesn't get into any trouble!" This chaplain, Captain, I'll call him Ch H, was a great mentor. On one occasion, the two of us went up into the student's dorm. When we entered, one of the student leaders called the room to attention—"room, ten hut!" Every man dropped what they were doing and stood at rigid attention. I had been around the military long enough and had seen enough movies to know what those words and actions meant. They meant that somebody important had entered. I looked around to see who it might be, not realizing it was us! Fortunately, Ch H knew what to do. He replied, "carry on!" and the men went back to their duties. I feel fortunate for me and those men that Ch H was there to give that response. There is no telling how long they would have held that position.

Ch H was a great officer and a great chaplain that cared for those he ministered. He was engaging and friendly to both students and instructors alike. He was a great role model. He was also endorsed by the Christian Science Church, one of the over 100 faith groups reflected in the U.S. Air Force Chaplain Corps. In many ways, our theology was miles apart and our worldview was vastly different. I was a Baptist minister, pastoring a small, very conservative church in south Texas. He was a Christian Science minister from southern California. Though we were different theologically, we had the same mission to care for Airmen. In fact, over the years I was there, on the staff of the Gateway Chapel were Baptists, Presbyterians, Lutherans, Catholics, and several other Christian Denominations. We also had a Rabbi and later an Imam on staff. How can such a wide spectrum of ministers not only get along, but also effectively minister? Probably the best word is "respect." Though theological conversations were inevitable, there was respect for each minister. We could minister shoulder to shoulder, not because we had a unified theological belief, rather because we had a unified mission.

This was a much different perspective than what I experienced back in the pastorate. In the local church, local ministers also respected one another; however, each church and for the most part, ministers in town stayed to themselves. Each minister had churches to pastor and the idea of an ongoing mission cooperation with other churches just didn't happen. "Besides," thought some, "if my kids get involved with the Baptists, they may like them better! We need all the bodies we can get!" So, I received my first taste of the Chaplaincy with the concept of "Cooperation without Compromise" firmly in place.

Another essential element was participating in the Worship Service, particularly being able to preach. The Gateway Chapel Sanctuary could hold over 2000 people. On Sundays, the General Protestant Service was filled to capacity with trainees and a few family members who had come for graduation that week. The service was unlike any other. It was full of joy and excitement—some Airmen were fueled by the Spirit of the Lord and others because they were out of sight and control of the Training Instructors! When I first preached at the Protestant Worship Service, I was impressed that so many had come to church. Perhaps they heard that Chaplain Marshall was preaching that day and made a special effort to come. I was quickly informed that the trainees had a choice—they could either come to worship or scrub the toilets! Hopefully, after hearing the sermon they left thinking they made the right choice!

Of course, I exaggerate! Airmen do have a choice. One of the roles of the military chaplain is to protect the Airmen's right to worship or not to worship. The chaplain has a focus on upholding the U.S. Constitution's First Amendment that states in part, "Congress shall make no law respecting an establishment of religion, or prohibiting the free exercise thereof…" There are two distinct "clauses" in this statement pertaining to Freedom of Religion. The first is the "Establishment Clause," meaning the government cannot establish a state religion. No one religion can be endorsed as an official religion. There is no "religion of the United States" or a "religion of the Air Force." The government, including the military cannot say, "you must worship this way." This concept and law benefits both the faith community and the nation as a whole. People are free to worship as they please. At Lackland, the largest worship service was the General Protestant Service. Simultaneously, on the other side of the Gateway Chapel was the Catholic Service. Smaller Worship Services, like Jewish, Muslim, and Buddhist services were also offered. Trainees without any faith background should not be required to attend any service. Chaplains, despite their personal faith background, assured that the trainees personal choices concerning religion or lack of were honored.

The second clause pertaining to Freedom of Religion is the "Free Exercise Clause." Though the government cannot establish or coerce religion on others, they cannot prohibit it as well.

Military members, no matter if they are in a training environment or not, are guaranteed the right to worship. One of the hallmarks of military chaplaincy is that chaplains go where the Soldiers/Sailors/Marines/Airmen go. Chaplains provide worship in comfortable chapels, on the battlefield, on the flightline, on ships, in small meeting rooms, no matter where military members may be. The worship experience is also free from any governmental interference. At Lackland and every base I preached, I would preach as if I was in my pastorate back home. Since this was a voluntary assembly for the purpose of worship, the service was solely in the hands of the chapel team, including the chaplain. A wise chaplain and chapel team will focus on the needs of the congregation and preach from texts and topics that meet them where they are on their spiritual journey.

A final, essential daily event for a chaplain is military

briefings—both providing and attending. I led two briefings on a regular basis. The first was an hour-long Chapel orientation for the trainees. In this, I would present some of the history of the chapel and the Chaplain Corps. This brief would emphasize the unique nature of chaplains who are both ministers (like their ministers back home) and military officers. I informed them that they would see chaplains at all levels of training as well as on their permanent duty station and deployments. I would emphasize our availability to counsel and that when speaking to a chaplain, the chaplain is bound to 100 percent confidentiality. More on this later. Simply, the briefing gave an overview of the work and availability of chaplain support while they were in training.

The second type of briefing was a bit more involved. Later in the six-week training schedule, Trainees would come to the chapel for an Adult Value Education Class (Later, Core Value Education)

led by the chaplain. This was a two-hour briefing. The purpose of this brief was to help teach good decision-making practices based on their core beliefs or values. The curriculum included several scenarios and utilized movie clips that would generate discussion. As a thirty-something Lieutenant, I loved leading these briefings. It was interesting to see the students' decision-making process and practical applications. To my dismay, I discovered that senior chaplain leadership decided this was not the role of the chaplain and that it would be given to military commanders. I was disappointed in the decision. It seemed very short-sided. If I could, I would have led a protest!

Years later, as a senior chaplain leader myself, I wholeheartedly concur with the decision. The class was addressing right behavior, but the chaplain could not give a theological foundation. Because this was a required formation, presenting this in a Bible-based format was not permitted, even if it was in the chapel building. Though some readers may balk at this, remember, in a military chapel like Lackland, there were not only Christian chaplains, but also Buddhist, Muslim, and Jewish chaplains on staff. Like the trainees, each of these chaplains came with their own world view and theological bias. Though this can be true of a military commander, the overlay of a religious component is removed. They can simply present a discussion of ethical behavior based on military expectations. Under the umbrella of religious freedom, chaplains, through worship or any other non-required gathering, can then offer a separate discussion on how moral and ethical decisions affect our behavior while giving a deeper, more spiritual theological base of understanding.

This experience was a great reminder, that whether in a civilian church or a military chapel, a good thing may not be the best thing. A clear focus is important. Another reminder, especially for younger chaplains, is that those who operate in a higher level sometimes have a perspective that those on the ground do not have. Of course, it is a reminder for senior chaplains, the opposite may be true as well!

As a reservist, I enjoyed the work I was able to do at Lackland. It provided a totally different opportunity to serve. Balancing the two worlds of civilian ministry and military chaplaincy was not always easy, but, as I have said many times, "I believe I was a better pastor because I was a chaplain and a better chaplain because I was a pastor."

There were crisis points along the way. A mere six months into my experience as a chaplain, a world event took place. On August 2, 1990, the nation of Iraq invaded and occupied Kuwait. The United States support which became Operation DESERT SHIELD had begun. Rumors began to swirl about future military involvement. One of the understandings of being a reservist is the awareness of being "called up." U.S. presidents have the authority to authorize a Presidential Reserve Call-up to augment U.S. Forces. This is known as an involuntary mobilization, meaning a member has no choice in the matter. As a reserve military member, I was vulnerable for this. I was assured; however, I had still had additional schools and training to attend. I would not be eligible for a call-up. The war escalated. Below gives a report of the events.

*Early on 17 January 1991, Operation desert shield
came to an end when the air campaign of Operation
desert storm began. Task Force normandy, consisting of
nine AH-64 Apache helicopters from the U.S. Army's
101st Aviation Regiment, 101st ABN DVN (Air Assault),
accompanied by four Air Force MH-53 Pave Low
special operations helicopters, flying fast and low,
opened fire at 0236—Baghdad time—on 17 January.
After their 27 Hellfire missiles destroyed Iraqi radar
sites, the Apaches followed with 100 Hydra-70 rockets
that knocked out the associated anti-aircraft guns. The
attack created a twenty-mile gap in the enemy's air
defense network opening a corridor through which U.S.
Air Force F-15E Strike Eagle fighters, supported by
EF-111 Ravens, raced into Iraqi air-space virtually
unopposed followed by hundreds of U.S. Air Force,
Navy, Marine Corps and Coalition fixed-wing aircraft
and cruise missiles.5*

Part of the new Operation DESERT STORM included a
ground war where mass casualties were predicted. Reservists
were called to serve. Despite assurances that I would not be on the
list, I received a letter on Valentines Day, February 14, 1991, that
indeed I was called to report to Lackland for a period of 365 days.
Though fifteen months prior, when I became a reservist, I knew
this was a possibility, I never really thought it would be a reality.
Given a couple of weeks to report, I began to inform my new
congregation and of course my family. On February 24th, the
ground war began. Remarkably, the campaign was overwhelming
for the Iraqi forces.

It was reported that:

> *In 100 hours, U.S. and allied ground forces in Iraq and*
>   *Kuwait decisively defeated a battle-hardened and*
> *dangerous enemy. During air and ground operations,*
> *U.S. and allied forces destroyed over 3,000 tanks, 1,400*
>   *armored personnel carriers, and 2,200 artillery pieces*
>   *along with countless other vehicles. This was achieved*
>   *at a cost to the United States of 96 soldiers killed in*
>   *action, 2 died of wounds, and 105 non-hostile deaths.*[6]

Because the need had diminished, on the Friday before my Monday report date, my mobilization orders were rescinded. In my 30 years of service, this was the first and only time I ever received an order of this type. It was definitely a wake-up call that my responsibility was not just to a handful of Airmen, but I was part of a much larger force.

DAY 1

Four-and-a-half hours into the nineteen-hour drive

Approaching Baton Rouge, Louisiana and having a strange sensation to say "Baton Rouge" in a Cajun accent, I was flooded with additional memories that helped shape me as a chaplain.

After 4 years of service, I pinned on the next rank of Captain. While at Lackland, I was given the opportunity to perform "special tours." In an attempt to broaden a chaplain's perspective beyond his/her local base, the Air Force Reserve Command provided alternate locations for Reserve personnel perform their annual tour. During the span of ten years while serving at Lackland, I performed two of these special tours—U.S. Air Force

Academy in Colorado Springs, CO and Nellis, AFB, Nevada.

The Air Force Academy (USAFA) tour was interesting because it gave me a greater understanding of elite officer training. The Academy is the "crown jewel" of the Air Force. Though these men and women were the same age as the trainees at Lackland, these "cadets" were select Air Force Academy students and would become Air Force officers. USAFA admission requirements are strict, competition is great, and the experience is intense. Those who graduate from the Academy are held in high esteem throughout their career. Part of their experience then and now is going through Basic Cadet Training at nearby Jack's Valley in the summer before their freshman year. Similar to the enlisted Basic Trainees, Cadets are led by enlisted instructors. These Cadets have upperclassmen Cadre that provide training and mentoring as well. Chaplains are available to fulfill their role to guarantee freedom of religion by providing worship, counseling, and visitation. They live and eat out in the field alongside the students and instructors.

The other tour took me outside of the entry-level military training environment and exposed me to the Air Combat Command (ACC) of the Air Force. The tour was in July, 1996. Nellis AFB is known for air combat exercises and is also the home to the Air Force Thunderbirds. The jets roaring across the base, resounding across the desert mountains, was an awesome sound.

Part of my experience at Nellis included participation in a military exercise called "Silver Flag Alpha" that involved the training of ground forces, (aka Security Forces.) In order to reach the location, a group of us drove an hour into the desert to the

Nellis Range. One of the Nellis Range Areas was Area 51 (though technically, there is no such area.) Of course, rumors of strange lights, aircraft, etc....were rampant. The exercise facility was a bare base located in the middle of a plateau desert. Sand blew incessantly. Temperatures hovered around 109 degrees. The training area embodied what I imagined when I "played Army" as a kid. There was a simulated weapons depot in the center of the base. On the perimeter, foxholes had been dug that contained two Airmen in each. In the exercise scenario, it was their responsibility to defend the base. As chaplains we talked with these Airmen in their individual foxholes dug into the thick sand. While wearing their protective gear, they appeared to be space aliens. Their gear included a canteen, radio, gas masks, backpacks, etc. Many wore thick motorcycle-type glasses beneath their helmets. They were covered from head to toe with sand. Each military member also wore a mylar vest with bumps protruding outward that would emit a beep when the member was hit by a laser emitting M-16. They were prepared for a simulated attack 24 hours a day.

At dusk, we joined the "aggressors" in the exercise for an attack. The same Airmen we were pastorally visiting earlier in the day would now be challenged. One of the best parts of this experience was the ability to wear night vision goggles. The moon was only a sliver, so visibility was low. Once donning these goggles, the darkened surrounding was illuminated with a green glow. We stealthily walked into the night toward the camp with the team leader and two young Airmen with M-16s strapped to their backs. As we were travelling through one of the wadis, the team leader stopped. He had detected a flare trap. Across the pass was a fine wire that had been attached to a warning flare. If the line had been pulled, a flare would have shot up illuminating our position. Each of us carefully stepped over the line. As the aggressors became closer, a firefight was about to ensue. Chaplains held back.

Far away from my training experience at Lackland, this training exercise was a dose of reality of war and its frightening uncertainty. This was not just "playing Army" with simulated situations and weapons, this was a realistic training to assist Airmen in real-world situations. It was also a reminder that the Air Force has ground forces. Not all of our work is on the flight line or behind a desk. The Air Force also deals with blowing sand, uncomfortable foxholes, and eating MREs (Prepacked Meals Ready to Eat.) Our small team finally left at midnight. I reluctantly turned in my $7000 night-vision goggles. I gave the incredibly clear night sky with its billions of stars a goodnight and began our trek back to our vehicles. Wait, what was that strange flash over Area 51?!

One of the chaplains who was involved with the combat training environment was Ch, Maj Charlie Bolin. Ch Bolin was also a Reserve Air Force chaplain. He was unlike any chaplain I had met at this point. Unlike most chaplains who were somewhat guarded and spoke in carefully chosen words, Ch Bolin was Mr. Personality. With his broad smile, engaging conversations, and his matter-of-fact outlook on life, he was immediately liked and loved by the Airmen he served. Part of his personality was reflected by his civilian occupation. He was employed by one of the hotels on the Las Vegas strip as a chaplain. He wasn't one of those "marryin' ministers" in some cheesy chapel, he was actually employed by a hotel whose manager was a former Army General. Like Gen Washington, the manager saw the value of having a minister available for his "troops" or in this case, his employees. Ch Bolin invited me to accompany him on one of his "religious engagements." In an environment far from the bleakness of the military field training environment a few miles away, the sights and sounds of the hotel casino were eye-popping and ear-deafening. The lights overhead were bright, the slot machines were chiming and dinging. The crowd of people was dense and loud. The sensory overload was almost unbearable!

Chaplain Bolin, now Chaplain Charlie, with his winsome smile moved around the hotel with ease. As comfortable as I saw him speaking to Airmen in the field, he had the same comfort with his hotel "congregation." Everybody he engaged seemed genuinely pleased to see him. One of the Casino supervisors told me that Charlie was a pillar of strength. Just like a local church pastor, Chaplain Charlie knew much about the people he served. He would ask questions concerning particular family members and followed up on previous prayer requests. Charlie also took me behind the scenes of the glitz and glamor of the flashing casino lights. There was a stark contrast as we moved to the service entrance just feet away from the noisy and busy casino. The noise was muffled, the walls were drab, and the tiled floor was plain. Charlie and I talked to one of the baggage handlers behind the front-desk wall. We then spoke with one of the security guards and toured monitors recording from the surveillance cameras that encompassed the facility. We engaged with bartenders who told of some family concerns, table dealers joking around, dancers that would give him a hug, etc…

Walking around with Chaplain Charlie gave me a totally different perspective of life in Las Vegas and the people who worked there. These were real people with real families with real problems. Though I may not understand or agree with every aspect of their lifestyle, this evening caused me to reflect upon the life of our Lord who became "flesh" and showed His love for us. He didn't just come for the "religious" people but for all, even those that we see on the fringes or those labeled "outcasts." This hotel on the strip was fortunate to have Ch Charlie. May he be an example for us all.

The highlight of the tour was on Wednesday of the final week of my duty at Nellis. I was able to join the crew of a KC-135 Stratotanker on a training mission high above the desert. This flying gas station can pump thousands of pounds of fuel to any capable aircraft, while flying thousands of feet above the ground. The Air National Guard crew from Ohio would be refueling A-10s, F-15s, and F-16s. Six of us entered the aircraft by climbing a 15-foot latter located under the nose of the plane. We walked by the air-conditioned cockpit to the back of the unairconditioned shell of the plane that served as the cargo bay. The floor was covered with steel rollers. The temperature was around 110 degrees. We sat in seats that extended the length of the plane.

The Flight Engineer informed us that the wind was too severe to take-off from this side of the flight line. After taxiing the entire length of the runway, we finally took off. The noise was deafening. After reaching 15,000 feet, the heat in the plane began to be more tolerable and we could see some smaller aircraft approaching. These aircraft were coming to refuel. The first group of aircraft were Fighter Jets—F-16s. On the KC-135, the "boom operator" lays on his stomach, propped up, and looks out window at the rear of the aircraft to extend his "boom" to the oncoming jets. I was able to position myself next to this operator, also propped up, on my belly. With the contours of the desert below providing the background, the fighter jets fell in line, waiting their turn, similar to any other vehicles waiting to refuel. The link-up between the two aircraft was a work of art as the boom operator extended his reach to the fuel receptor on the nose of the jet. After they received their fuel and departed, a group of aircraft known as A-10s arrived. As before, the aircraft below seemed so close—in fact, they were a mere 47 feet away. I felt I could just reach out and touch them. After refueling, many of the pilots would give a salute of thanks and would quickly depart.

This experience was remarkable and just one mission of our incredible Air Force.

As mentioned, the life of a reservist is a balancing act—balancing Air Force life, church life, and family life. After my tour at Nellis, "Operation FAMILY VACATION" commenced! I had driven from our home in Stockdale, Texas to Las Vegas, Nevada. Before the trip, I stuffed the back of our Ford minivan with luggage. On Saturday morning, after my two-week tour, my wife, Susie; son, Blake; and daughter, Amanda boarded an airplane to Las Vegas. Blake was eleven years old; Amanda was nine. Long before airport security measures resulting from 9/11, I greeted my family at the gate. Though I had only been gone two weeks, the reunion was memorable. Both kids ran and embraced me. My wife gave me a hug and a kiss and the west to east vacation had begun. It was a whirlwind. We began by staying one night in Las Vegas and watching a magic show. We then headed to Hoover Dam, followed by the Grand Canyon.

We continued eastward to Four Corners and Mesa Verde. We then went to Durango, CO and boarded the Durango and Silverton Railroad. It was great, although we were covered in soot! We commenced to Albuquerque NM and rode the Sandia Peak Tramway, the world's largest tram, then to Alamogordo NM and Holloman AFB followed by White Sands National monument. Finally, in Texas, we traveled through El Paso, San Angelo, and eventually found our way back to Stockdale. It was good to be home! For me, it took a while to soak in all I had been a part for the past three and a half weeks. It was a summer to remember!

DAY 1

Seven hours into the nineteen-hour drive

Continuing eastward, I entered Mobile, AL. I was getting a bit tired but was determined to press on to the Florida Panhandle. After a couple of stops for food and gas, the cat, still somewhat calm, and I continued down the road.

I spent ten years serving at Lackland along with two special tours and various conferences and training events. If it were up to me, I would have stayed at Lackland. The ministry was readily available and extremely rewarding. From the time I arrived at the base to the time I left, I was actively engaged. Since the trainees rotated every six weeks, they simply saw me as one of the chaplains, not a reservist who had come for his duty. There was nothing on my uniform that distinguished me from any Active-Duty chaplain. I was able to be available to these Airmen as they journeyed through the difficult Basic Training process. After Basic Training, these graduates were sent to a "Tech School" to learn and hone their military job. These bases are located throughout the United States. One of the Tech Trainings located at Lackland was designed for Security Forces—the same career field I had gotten acquainted with at Nellis. I was able to minister to these students as well. Because Tech Training environment provided more freedom for the students, Sunday worship attendance was much lower. Unit religious engagements and counseling continued. Ministry remained fruitful and meaningful.

After spending a decade assigned to Lackland, the Air Force Command Chaplain Corps leadership decided it was time for me to move on to another assignment. I had recently pinned on the rank of Major and my Air Force aperture needed to be widened. I didn't go far, simply across the city of San Antonio to Randolph Air Force Base. Randolph, though still a training base for pilots, was more similar to other Air Force Chapel communities. The base offered a variety of programs for children, youth, and adults. On Sunday morning, instead of seeing a sea of camouflaged Airmen, these participants wore civilian clothes and the vast majority of them were civilian. At the time this was commonplace in the majority of stateside Air Force Chapels. The Air Force chaplain had two distinct groups to minister—the Airmen and their families during the week with the addition of retirees and their families on Sunday.

Randolph has a beautiful and historic chapel building. As described in Joint Base San Antonio News (JBSA), "Built in the image of Missions Concepción and San Jose in San Antonio, the main chapel at Joint Base San Antonio-Randolph has served the spiritual needs of the base community since it was completed in 1934.... it's one of the great buildings on Randolph to visit if you want to see historic architecture in almost pristine state. This is a historic base with a historic campus and the chapel is very much like it was in 1934 when it was opened originally...the structure is distinguished by its six stained-glass windows—none of them original to the building—and its "rose window" that, like the structure itself, hearkens back to the Spanish colonial period."[7]

The historic chapel has always been a favorite location for weddings. JBSA News also records, "One of the little-known facts about the chapel is that some of the leading figures in the Air

Force's history have been married there, including Maj. Thomas McGuire. McGuire died for his country in early 1945. He was the second leading ace in Air Force history, and other aces have been married there as well. We don't have a direct catalog of all the main events and some of the large funerals and weddings that have happened there, but when you look at the history of Randolph, which is now almost 90 years old, you feel kind of a wave of history when you go in the chapel."[8]

Weddings at the chapel were not only popular in the 1940s, they were popular in the 2000s as well. Active-Duty chaplains, assigned to the chapel were called upon to conduct these weddings. A requirement for most chaplains was some sort of pre-marriage counseling. One of my major projects in helping "augment" the force was developing and implementing a pre-marriage weekend that lasted from Friday night to Saturday afternoon. This enabled the necessary counseling while freeing up the Active-Duty chaplain to focus on the details of the actual ceremony. All Protestant couples who desired to be married at the Randolph Chapel were required to go through my pre-marriage weekend event.

I have found that in both civilian and military settings, the bride-to-be is almost always excited to be a part of marriage preparation weekends like this. Grooms-to-be seemed to universally dread them! So, to appeal to them and make it more inviting for the men, the theme of my marriage preparation weekend was "Home Improvement." I noted that building a home is an enormous challenge. Unlike a house that is built and maintained, homebuilding is a lifelong process that continually requires extensive work. The repeated phrase was, "Building the home God desires utilizes solid plans, a firm foundation, and quality building materials."

Solid plans focused on Proverbs 24:3-4, "By wisdom a house is built and by understanding it is established and by knowledge the rooms are filled with all precious and pleasant riches." The foundation focused on Matthew 7:24-2. We talked about foundation crumblers like busyness, irritability, boredom, drift, debt, and pain from the past. We discussed the quality of building materials of commitment, communication, negotiation, intimacy, and vision. Various Scriptures were weaved throughout with references to well-known marriage enrichment speakers and authors. We also utilized a wide range of videos. In the intimacy section, I included a "Self-Quiz for Lovers." Some of the questions looking for a true or false answer were: "I believe that love at first sight occurs between two people," and "I believe that if my spouse really loves me, he/she will always know what I want or need to be happy," and "I believe that infidelity can occur in marriage even if there is no sexual intercourse."

I concluded the weekend with the section on vision utilizing Ecclesiastes 3:1, "There is an appointed time for everything. And there is a time for every event under heaven." I added, sometimes we live "East of Eden" in a world where people are scarred and broken by sin, yet God has given us the resources to overcome in each season of life. We cannot stop the winds of the world from blowing, but we can build upon a firm foundation. We can utilize the building resources that God has provided. Unlike physical houses that deteriorate with age, our personal homebuilding can grow stronger as we put our full confidence in God, the Master-builder." And finally, "You are not alone! Rely on Faith, Family, Friends, and Resources (speakers, weekends, books, etc..)

The Pre-Marriage weekend seemed to be impactful. Even the men participated! Marriage in the military can be stressful. Hopefully, the weekend sparked some interest and inspiration as they entered into this important time in their lives. (See Flight Notes #1.)

As an outgrowth of the pre-marriage weekend, the Randolph Wing Chaplain requested that I develop and lead a marriage retreat for married couples, one of whom was a military member who had recently returned from a deployment. This provided an opportunity for couples to re-connect and renew their relationship. This training was not held at the chapel, rather, in a more romantic setting—a hotel at the San Antonio Riverwalk (See Flight Notes #2.)

Ministry at Randolph was unique from Lackland, but just as fruitful. Along with the Pre-Marriage weekends, I conducted several funerals—some at the chapel, some graveside ceremonies at the national cemetery at Ft. Sam Houston. I also conducted weddings, and invocations at retirements and other events. I had several opportunities for religious engagements on the flightline, workstations, and inside the walls of the chapel. I was also exposed, in a greater manner, to the work of chaplain assistants. Chaplain assistants are enlisted members who provide logistics and administrative assistance. When I first became exposed to the Chaplaincy, their role, at least from my perspective, was very limited. Over the years, they were rightfully given much more responsibility and direct involvement in ministering to Airmen. As members of the Chaplain Service (later the name was changed to "Chaplain Corps"), their contribution was invaluable. A chaplain and chaplain assistant were seen as a "RST," a Religious Support Team. I served with pride beside these men and women who desired to provide ministry excellence.

One more story on Randolph that reveals my humanity. There is a certain picture that the average person has about an Air Force officer, especially a Field Grade officer, Major and above. He/she is seen as polished and professional, never seemingly fazed in crisis moments. At least, that is how it is in Hollywood! In reality, our mind does not always work correctly, and yes, we do dumb things.

I can give one example. During this time, I had been called to pastor a church in Dickinson, TX, which increased my travel time to the base to 3 and a half hours. When I would perform my duty at Lackland or Randolph, it was common for me to leave after Wednesday night prayer meeting in Dickinson and drive through the night, arriving after midnight. I would then work at the base on Thursday and Friday to be back at the church on Sunday. So, on this particular trip, I arrived at the base late on Wednesday night, got up early on Thursday, and worked throughout the day. On Thursday evening, I was ready to get back to the government billeting and go to bed early. So, I walked into my room with government beeper (I was on call and beepers were still a thing.) Later that evening, just about the time I was going to bed, I heard a single beep. My first thought was my beeper, but it didn't have a steady, loud sound. I waited a few seconds, and I heard it again, one single beep. I knew this sound. Just a few days prior, at my house, the smoke alarm detector had the same sound. The battery needed to be replaced and a steady, intermittent stream of beeps was heard. This is one of the mysteries of smoke detectors. I have rarely had a battery go bad during the day. The obnoxious beep always comes at night, sometimes in the middle of the night, resounding across the room. Knowing what to do, I stood on the swivel bar chair that was in the room (not smart!) and dislodged the smoke detector from the ceiling and removed the battery. Solved, at least for the night. As I was descending the chair, I heard the sound again and noticed a carbon monoxide detector. I was unable to dislodge that one.

My next step was to call the VOQ (Visiting Officer's Quarters) front desk. I explained my predicament, with a bit of frustration. They informed me that no maintenance personnel would be available until the morning. Resigned to the situation, I made the best of it. I pretended that the beep, which would occur around every 45 seconds was not a big deal. Certainly, I could ignore it and sleep through it. Even with a pillow over my head, my sleep that night was spotty at best.

The next day, with the steady beep still present, I got up and readied myself for the day's work. I gathered my notebook and beeper and walked out the door. When I entered the stairwell, to my utter astonishment, I heard a beep. Since the beep had been resonating throughout the room, I was unaware, until this point, that the bad battery was actually in the beeper all along. I felt a bit foolish that I didn't discover this until the morning. When I got to the chapel office, I called the front desk and told them not to send anyone to the room, that the problem was fixed. The front office young lady was relentless. She was the epitome of customer service and wanted to ensure that everything was fine and continued to ask a series of questions. Finally, I admitted my mistake. She laughed.

I recall this story because it reminds me of who I am, despite the nice rank and pressed uniform. Underneath it all, I'm just a guy. I'm a guy who misplaces his keys at times, breaks something in the house and glues it back before my wife knows, loads the dishwasher incorrectly, and forgets to put down the toilet seat. I'm just a guy. Though I have some distinct, and to some impressive roles and responsibilities, at the end of the day I am simply one of God's children who deals with life's troubles, trials, and triumphs like the next guy.

I can also be a bit mischievous. I mentioned the chapel office. In the office was a 72-year-old retiree, a female secretary who had worked there for years. Behind her desk was a work area separated by a sliding glass window. By that window was a copier and a shredder. I had some documents that needed to be shredded, so I was running them through the machine. Since her desk was just a few feet away and the shredder was incredibly noisy, it was obvious what I was doing. I decided to have a little fun. I stopped, went to her desk, and with a straight face asked, "Edna, I am trying to run these copies, but they don't seem to be coming out." She looked at me with a look that could have been accompanied with a "Oh, bless your heart." In a Southern context, that usually means, "You are so dumb!" She tried to say something, but the words just stuck in her throat. I quickly assured her that I was just joking. Her laugh was much more subtle than the VOQ front desk laugh.

9/11

Though I was not on duty at the time, it was during this time period, September 11, 2001, when four coordinated attacks from highjacked Airlines shocked the United States and the world. Two of the planes slammed into New York's Twin towers, causing both to collapse. Another struck the Pentagon. A final attack was averted when passengers forced the hijackers to crash the plane near Shanksville, PA.

The attacks shook America to the core. Questions like "how could this happen?" and "what is going to happen next?" and "what should we do?" were rampant. On the evening of 9/11, President George Bush announced that the US would "make no distinction between terrorists who committed these acts and those who harbor them."[9]

With a flurry of domestic support and the world in its favor, the 107th Congress passed on 18 September 2001 a Joint Resolution to authorize the use of the United States Armed Forces against those responsible for the recent attacks launched against the United States. The "War on Terror," officially, the Global War on Terrorism (GWOT) had begun.

Military assets were put on alert, including Reserve Forces. President George Bush said it succinctly, "The message is for everybody who wears the uniform: The United States will do what it takes to win this war."[10] 11,000 Air Force Reservists were mobilized by March 2002. It was the action that solidified the statement made by the AFRC Commander, Lieutenant General James E. Sherrard III, "We are not just the back-up team."[11] Indeed, Total Force was at full implementation.

Much has been written and discussed about 9/11; including the initial shock, the wave of patriotism, the political and military response, and the resulting changes in our nation's security.

Behind every news headline there was a story of personal pain and anguish, including one that hit close to home. On that fateful day, one of the casualties was a high school (Judson High School) classmate of mine. Her name was Karen Wagner. In 2004, the Judson Independent School District, in Converse, TX named its second high school in honor of Karen Wagner.

Her story was recorded by KSAT-12 News in San Antonio on September 11, 2021, exemplified many who died that day:

"San Antonio has many connections to the 9/11 terrorist attacks and one of them is the story of U.S. Army LTC Karen Wagner. Wagner graduated from Judson High School in 1979. She was the third of four children and came from a military family.

Wagner was a popular student and star athlete, but also well known in the community as someone who was always willing to help those in need.

'She definitely was a very fun spirit, very athletic, the type of person who had three pennies, she would give you two,' said Anthony Cristo, English II World Literature teacher at Wagner High School. 'That whole family is just good people. They have a sense of honor. They have a sense of duty.'

Wagner carried her passion to help others to college. She went to the University of Nevada, Las Vegas and became a distinguished military graduate, later earning her master's degree in health services administration back in San Antonio.

She was commissioned in 1984 as a medical service corps officer. Her assignments included duties at Fort Sam Houston and Walter Reed Army Medical Center in Washington, D.C. 'Knowing what contributed to the Walter Reed hospital among many other things, it's just I'm honored to know that what she did for us and for our military,' said Anne Ream, World History and Mexican American Studies teacher at Wagner High School. In the summer of 2001, Wagner had just been promoted to the rank of Lieutenant Colonel. The unthinkable happened months later on Sept. 11.

LTC Wagner was in the Pentagon, working in her cubicle, when a hijacked plane crashed into the building. Without hesitation, Karen stepped in to try and help save others. She died in the attack, but her legacy has lived on. The lives of some teachers at Wagner, many of them veterans themselves, were shaped by that day. Anthony Cristo was a Navy Corpsman, but also served in the 4th Light Armored Reconnaissance Marines. 'She died trying to help others get out of the Pentagon when it hit,' said Cristo. 'It's a tragedy that we lost her and at the same time, that was possibly part of the impetus for me to enlist in the military. 'Paul Fenoglio, a math and computer science teacher at Wagner High School, served in the U.S. Army. 'She died trying to help some people escape the fires at the Pentagon, sacrificing herself for others,' said Fenoglio. 'And our students said, what that should mean to us is we should look beyond ourselves. How can we serve others? We want students to look beyond themselves to what their mission in life is. That's what Karen Wagner means to me. I'm glad they named the school after, but I wish they didn't have to,' said Cristo. 'I know that the way Karen died should be noted. But also, her life is something that we should emulate and cherish.'"[12]

The Global War on Terrorism that followed greatly affected training and awareness The war went on to cost thousands of lives, including more than 2,000 American Service members and trillions of dollars in military spending. The shadow of this war was present throughout the remainder of my military career.

DAY 1

Eleven and a half hours into the nineteen-hour drive

The sun was beginning to set. I was somewhere on the outskirts of Tallahassee, Fl in the Florida Panhandle. This portion of the trip was about to end. Time to rest and hit the road again tomorrow.

DAY 2

Still Eleven and a half hours into the nineteen-hour drive

I woke up the next morning realizing I was in the state of Florida but was still 8 hours away from my destination! Still on I-10, will soon be headed south on I-90. The cat is resigned to this long trip. Off we go with more memories.

In 2006, after spending 6 years at Randolph, it was time for another move. My place of attachment (assignment) was now at the Air Force Reserve Command (AFRC) Headquarters at Robins AFB, GA in the Command Chaplain office. This is an office I would know very well in the coming years. For now, I was still an IMA, a part-time reservist. Though I did fulfill one annual tour at the office, it was not the focus of the new assignment. I was designated to be part of the Chaplain cadre at the Patriot Defender Exercise at Camp Swift, TX followed by Camp Gruber in Oklahoma.

AFRC hosted a training for its Reserve Security Forces members at these sites. It provided sustainment and qualification training. The in-field Security Forces training allowed Security Forces personnel to become proficient with weapons as well as learn about new technologies. The training encompassed one-hundred twenty-three hours including forty hours of Field Training Exercise.

This training, which was established in 1998, was conducted in five two-week increments. Training was provided by the 610th Security Forces (SF) Squadron from Carswell AFB, Texas. In the 2008 fiscal year, each of the SF participants were scheduled for an overseas deployment in support of the Global War on Terrorism. Like Silver Flag Alpha, the Security Forces Airmen received critical pre-deployment training. The training included land navigation, mounted and dismounted tactics, patrolling, urban operations, and basic medical techniques.

A maximum of one-hundred thirty-two Security Forces students were onsite for each Patriot Defender rotation. Because of the intensity of the program, leadership from AFRC Security Forces requested a Chaplain Corps presence—normally three to six personnel (chaplains and chaplain assistants,) to support this training. AFRC Chaplain Corps leadership agreed. The opportunity opened a door of expanded ministry. Not only would Chaplain Corps members be available to provide ministry to the Security Forces personnel, training for deployment ministry would also be provided for chaplains and chaplain assistants. For the Chaplain Corps, it was both an opportunity to minister and an opportunity to expose members to deployment conditions.

The chaplain leader of this project was Ch Charlie Bolin, my friend from Las Vegas. I was brought onto the team to develop and teach a leadership track. The focal point of the training was an examination of the unique leadership challenges and opportunities in a highly diverse and pluralistic military environment.

During the two-week training, Chaplain Corps members were exposed to deployment exercise scenarios and practiced some of the leadership skills learned. Through training and application, they were shown how effective spiritual, moral, and ethical leadership could become a significant force multiplier at the Patriot Defender exercise and could serve as a model for the entire USAF Chaplain Corps. The partnership of Security Forces and Chaplain Corps proved to be mutually beneficial. Working alongside the Security Forces in a deployed setting enabled a unique perspective. Chaplains and chaplain assistants were not only able to identify with the warrior Airmen, but they also learned security measures that provided training for their own protection.

An important aspect of the training was the need to build

teamwork strengthened by strong communication skills. The chaplains not only worked together in this deployed environment, they also slept, ate, and commiserated together. They were expected to deal with several stressors during this two-week exercise. Physically they faced the elements of the weather, sometimes extreme heat or cold. They accompanied their Security Forces squadrons on foot and mounted patrols. They fought through the tangled brush during the compass orientation training. They learned the importance of water hydration and food intake. They learned to like or at least tolerate the taste of MREs. Emotionally, they dealt with irritability, homesickness, and anxiety. They coped with all of this while being expected to minister to the Airmen and form a cohesive team with the other Chaplain Corps members—both chaplain and chaplain assistants.

This kind of training cannot be replicated in a classroom experience alone. Though two weeks is far from ideal, it gave a taste of what deployment ministry entails. This "incarnational" ministry gave tremendous credibility to those the Chaplain Corps members were called to serve. The United States Air Force and the nation it represents desperately needs then and now to hear the spiritual, moral, and ethical voice of the dedicated, equipped chaplain. (See Flight Notes #3.)

Of all career fields that I have worked with, Security Forces was the most common. I ministered to them at Lackland on a regular basis and during my two-week tour at Nellis. Those experiences were in a very condensed timeframe. At the Patriot Defender exercise, I was totally immersed in their world. In many ways, I was in a different world from my church life. First, the living conditions and the scenarios we participated in were much different than back home. Before I became an instructor, I participated in Patriot Defender as a student. I particularly remember a Sunday morning at 11:00am when I normally would have been in the pulpit preaching in a nice, air-conditioned sanctuary. On this day, I was being "protected" by Security Forces while in a building that was becoming overrun with the "aggressor force." Chaplains are non-combatants and are not permitted to even touch a weapon. So, it was the place of the chaplain assistant, who was armed and Security Forces to protect. As the noise of "simunitions" and smoke filled the air, I thought of how far I was from the local church…and knowing I was not in any real danger, how much fun this really was!

I was also impressed with these young Security Forces members. The days included carrying their weapon and wearing their uniform—BDUs and the recent change of uniform in the Air Force, ABUs (Airman Battle Uniforms.) In the evening, the Airmen could wear their PT (Physical Training) gear—blue shorts and t-shirt. Even in these more casual uniforms, they carried their weapons, ready for a simulated attack. With these young faces, I could not help but think about my church experiences of going to church youth camp. As the Airmen lined-up to eat in the Dining Hall, they looked like any other church camp members, except for, of course their automatic rifles carried across their shoulder!

Language in these trainings was different from my church world as well. For whatever reason, their language was pretty ripe! I never really liked people holding their tongue around me solely because I was a minister and a chaplain. I know it was out of respect, but when they said, "sorry, chaplain" I felt like they were apologizing to their mom! Security Forces, at least those in this environment, just let it loose. Their favorite word was the "F" word. Once when I was riding with a member in a vehicle I came out and asked, "Why do so many Security Forces use the 'F' word?" It seems kind of limiting. You should be more imaginative and use a variety of words." He just looked at me. I don't think he expected me to challenge him on his language and certainly didn't expect me to encourage him to broaden his vocabulary! The main point of that conversation was to encourage him to at least think about what he was saying and maybe even move to words that were more uplifting.

This also brings up a point of chaplain interaction. Some chaplains are so comfortable behind the stained-glass windows that they hardly ever emerge and expose themselves to the raw world. People respect them, but they cannot relate to them. Other chaplains are so immersed with their culture that their language and lifestyle are no different from the rest of the men and women they serve. People can relate to them, but rarely respect them. Somewhere, in between these two extremes is the sweet spot where the chaplain is theologically, morally, and ethically sound but also is able to relate to the community they serve.

Interacting and getting to know fellow Chaplain Corps members who were going through the training was enjoyable. It was great to have time to discuss their lives, their goals, and future plans. And, of course, Ch Bolin always made things interesting.

DAY 2

Seventeen hours into the nineteen-hour drive

Palm Trees are becoming more and more common.

The reality of a new ministry in a new location in an intense military environment was beginning to sink in. How did this happen? What made me uproot my familiar surroundings?

Earlier, in the Spring of 2008, I attended the Wing Chaplain Course at Maxwell AFB, AL. This is the third of three courses required for chaplains. Since I was a newly pinned-on Lt Col, I was fulfilling this requirement. At the course, Ch, Col Jeff Dull, the Command Chaplain at the United States Southern Command (USSOUTHCOM) stated that he was looking for a new Deputy. He needed a reservist with the rank of Lt Col. My first thought was, "Moving to Miami—that would be awesome!" My next thought was, "There is no way I would ever move to Miami!" After talking with him and with the recommendation of the AFRC Command Chaplain, Ch, Col Don Smith, I put my name in the hat. This was not the first time that I submitted my name for a position. I simply kept the door open with no real expectations. If offered, I could easily say "no."

USSOUTHCOM is a joint environment—meaning it is composed of several military services. Ch Dull was casting the net wide across the various military services to determine the right choice. Surprisingly, in mid-summer, I received a call that the job was mine, if I desired. I had already talked with Susie about this potential move. So, after the call, I went home and asked her, "What do you think about moving to Miami?" Her response, "Are you moving to Miami?" I replied, "I have been offered the position, so I guess…yes." Her response, "If you are moving to Miami, I am moving to Miami!"

You gotta love it! I began the process of informing the church, informing friends and family, and preparing to sell a house we had spent the last ten years. To top it off, during this time, a major hurricane hit the Texas gulf coast. We were leaving the familiar behind and preparing ourselves for a full-time military position in the strange new world of south Florida. I am now at the threshold of a new opportunity and challenge.

DAY 2

Nineteen hours into the nineteen-hour drive

I have arrived! The cat and I are both relieved. The three-year USSOUTHCOM adventure is about to begin. Though I remain a member of the Air Force Reserve, I will be in full-time status for the next 1095 days.

United States Southern Command

A New Stratosphere

Though I had been in the military for the past 20 years, my arrival at the United States Southern Command (USSOUTHCOM or more commonly referred to as: SOUTHCOM) was somewhat daunting. I felt like it was my first day in grade school. I was wearing the proper uniform with lunch packed in my backpack. I stood before a two-story brick building that resembled an office building; in fact it was an office building. Except for the big "United States Southern Command" signage and obvious security, it looked like any other large corporate office. The SOUTHCOM headquarters was miles away from the closest military installation. The building was located in Doral, a town on the outskirts of Miami. Personnel included over 2,800 people representing all branches of the Armed Forces, 13 federal agencies and representatives from six partner nations.

Interestingly enough, the building was directly across the street from the Doral Country Club, where the infamous (at least for professional golf fans) 18th hole was dubbed, "The Blue Monster."

SOUTHCOM is one of six "Geographic Combatant Commands." A Geographic Combatant Command is a joint military command of the United States Department of Defense. It is composed of units from two or more service branches and conducts broad and continuing missions in distinct Geographic areas.

The six Geographic Combatant Commands are:

- USAFRICOM: U.S. Africa Command, Kelley Barracks, Stuttgart, Germany.
- USCENTCOM: U.S. Central Command, MacDill Air Force Base, FL.
- USEUCOM: U.S. European Command, Patch Barracks, Stuttgart, Germany.
- USNORTHCOM: U.S. Northern Command, Peterson Air Force Base, CO.
- USINDOPACOM: U.S. Indo-Pacific Command, Camp H.M. Smith, HI.
- USSOUTHCOM: U.S. Southern Command, Miami, FL.[1]

Each Combatant Command has an "Area of Responsibility" (AOR.) Each Combatant Command (COCOM) commander—a four-star General Officer—is responsible to the President of the United States and the Secretary of Defense to conduct operations in their particular AOR. SOUTHCOM is responsible for U.S. military operations, cooperation and partnership-building in a region that includes 31 countries and 10 territories in the Caribbean, Central America and South America. This represents one half billion people. To assist in this, the commander relies on a robust staff of "Subject Matter Experts" (SMEs) in the areas of personnel, planning, operations, communication, logistics, etc...as well as special staff such as legal, medical, public affairs, and of course, chaplain.

In walking through the high security doors of the Southern Command, I have entered into a new stratosphere of the military. I have moved from the "tactical" to the "strategic" level of operations. Though I still wear a cross on my uniform and I would still conduct weddings and funerals, assist in providing death notifications, and pastoral counseling, these were not my main tasks.

As the Deputy Command Chaplain, I would be responsible to assist the Command Chaplain in his responsibilities. As noted in the Southern Command website:

"The Command Chaplain is the primary advisor to the commander on religion, ethics and morals. The Command Chaplain is responsible for coordinating chaplain support to ensure the free exercise of religion for Army, Navy, Air Force, Marine and Coast Guard service members, their family members and other U.S. personnel within the SOUTHCOM area of responsibility (AOR). The chaplain also serves as liaison with civilian and military religious organizations and leaders in the AOR"[2]

Some distinctives that were unique in this environment

1. As mentioned, the work was at the strategic level coordinating resources from all military services, civilians, and non-DoD personnel. In the headquarters building, the number of personnel was the size of a Texas megachurch.
2. SOUTHCOM, like all Combatant Commands, was very rank-heavy. The SOUTHCOM Commander was a Four-Star Officer, the Deputy Commander was a Three-

Star Officer, the Chief of Staff was a Two-Star Officer, each of the Directors on Staff were led One- or Two-Star Officers or O-6 (in the Air Force, this rank is Colonel.) The enlisted included many senior level ranks as well. These Active-Duty senior leaders normally fulfilled a three-year tour. Being a Joint Command, their replacement was from a different military service. Toward the end of my tour, Chaplain Dull (Air Force) was replaced by Chaplain King (Navy.) Though I would have rooms called to attention as a First Lieutenant at Lackland, as a Lt Col at SOUTHCOM, my rank was barely given a nod.

3. The size of the Chaplain's office was distinct. In my previous assignments, I was part of a medium to large staff. At SOUTHCOM, the full-time staff was four—the Command Chaplain, Deputy Command Chaplain, Senior Enlisted, and at a later date, a civilian Administrative Assistant. Though the office was small, the responsibility was huge. Between manning the office when the Command Chaplain traveled, to my travels to various locations, to engaging with personnel, to examining chaplain plans, and countless other duties, my days were full.

4. My travel time to and from the office increased. Susie and I settled in an apartment north of Miami and west of Ft. Lauderdale in a town called Weston. With traffic, it was about a forty-five-minute drive. Several SOUTHCOM personnel lived in Weston and most days I was part of a transportation "van pool."

LEARNING CURVE

There is an expression that is fitting to most new assignments, especially to one like SOUTHCOM, "it's like drinking out of a firehose." I was thirsty to learn, but I was not that thirsty! It took some time to absorb the myriad of paperwork and briefings: Air

Force Element in-processing checklists, various Air Force and DoD forms, Household goods (HHG) moving forms, etc…One step I had never taken until this point in my Air Force career was the move to obtain a TS/SCI Security clearance. I would move from "Secret" to "Top Secret." This clearance would allow me to enter various areas for visitation. It would also allow me to view military plans as needed. A full investigation took place to receive this clearance. I would be interviewed. My background would be investigated as well as my credit score. The process also included personal interviews with those I knew. I found out later that a couple of people from Dickinson received a call and a visit. I guess I passed the investigation because I eventually received my clearance!

The firehose learning continued with learning every functional area of the Headquarters. Terminology was diverse. Instead of Air Force terms that I knew well, I also learned Army, Navy, Marine, and Coast Guard terminology—some official and some unofficial! Learning ranks from various services, especially Navy ranks took a bit of effort. In this Joint environment, good-natured kidding took place as well. Some differences were noted. For example, it was allowable for a member of the Air Force to hold an umbrella outside in the rain. Sounds sensible, but holding an umbrella was not allowed for the Marines. They would simply bear the elements and become soaked in the process. (In 2019, this policy was changed allowing Marines to carry all black, collapsible umbrellas during inclement weather with the service and dress blue uniforms. I have been told that younger Marines welcomed the change. Older members have mixed opinions—some welcoming and some grumbling. Marines who have always been proud of their amphibious nature are now part of the umbrella club!) Speaking of Marines, I have heard, "never ask someone if they are a Marine. If they are, they will tell you. If not, why embarrass them?

Particularly in the field, and sometimes in a briefing, you could hear a Service-specific battle cry. Normally, it is used to respond to a verbal greeting or as an expression of enthusiasm. Battle cries vary by Service. Marines use the phrase, "Oorah," Army uses the phrase, "Hooah," and the Navy and Coast Guard occasionally use the phrase, "Hooyah." Though you may hear an Air Force member use a battle cry, it normally comes from someone who was previously in another Branch of Service. To the rest of the services, an appropriate Air Force battle cry may be a Matthew McConaughey themed, "Alright, Alright, Alright!" Personally, I think a spirited "Hallelujah" response could be implemented by all!

In 2009, during my time at SOUTHCOM, the Navy changed their "Navy Working Uniform" to a Blue Digital Camouflage. The Army and Air Force also changed to a digital wooded camouflage or desert uniform designed to blend into a hostile environment. It didn't seem to make a lot of sense for a member of the Navy to wear a uniform that provided camouflage in the water. If a Navy member is in the water, he/she is in trouble. "Man overboard" and "a watery blue camouflage uniform did not seem to go hand in hand! (This uniform, also known as "blueberry," was discontinued in 2019.)

Service comparisons have been part of the military culture for some time. An old joke describes how to tell the difference between the Services: If you give the command, "Secure the Building", here is what the different services would do:

Secure the Building! The Navy would turn out the lights and

lock the doors.

Secure the Building! The Army would surround the building with defensive fortifications, tanks, and concertina wire.

Secure the Building! The Marines would assault the building, using overlapping fields of fire from all appropriate points on the perimeter.

Secure the Building! The Air Force would take out a three-year lease with an option to buy!

We can't forget the Coast Guard. The U.S. Coast Guard operates under the U.S. Department of Homeland Security during peacetime. During times of war, it can be transferred in whole or in part to the U.S. Department of the Navy under the Department of Defense by order of the U.S. President or by act of Congress.

Prior to its transfer to Homeland Security, it operated under the Department of Transportation from 1967 to 2003 and the Department of the Treasury from its inception until 1967.[3]

Their placement in the Department of Homeland Security allows law enforcement powers unlike other branches of the military which are prevented by law to engage in law enforcement capacities.[4]

Coast Guard personnel play a pivotal part of the mission of SOUTHCOM and are an integral part of the total SOUTHCOM team.

Along with the various Services, SOUTHCOM had a variety of civilian employees working in military missions. It also hosted several other non-DoD federal agencies.

The totality of these personnel represented "TEAM SOUTHCOM." Military members from various Services and a civilian force working side by side to meet the needs of the mission at hand. It was a pleasure to serve with these incredibly intelligent, talented, and devoted men and women on a daily basis.

A TIME TO WEEP...AND REJOICE

Early in 2009, my mom passed away in Houston, TX. Part of the difficult decision to leave Texas was knowing that my mother was in poor health. She was under great care at an assisted living facility with my sister and brother-in-law nearby. I had truly sensed the Lord's leading to make this move and my family, including my mom, was supportive. On her last day, I was able to speak with her while my sister held the phone to her ear. That call is precious to me. It gave me an opportunity to hear her voice and tell her once more how much I loved her. She died shortly after. After making work arrangements, Susie and I boarded a flight from Ft. Lauderdale to San Antonio, where the memorial service would be held. She would then be buried at the National Cemetery at Ft. Sam Houston, TX where my father was buried. It was a difficult but sweet time as Susie and I gathered with my sister, brother-in-law, their children, my children and a host of church members to remember and honor her. She was extremely proud of her family and left a legacy of faith behind. In honor of her life, allow me to share her obituary:

"June Elizabeth Marshall (Betty) was born May 12, 1930, to Guy and Hazel Duckett in Newport News, Va. And went home to be with the Lord on March 29, 2009, in Houston, Tx. "Home" was always an important part of Betty's life. She enjoyed the home of her childhood in Newport News with her parents, her sister, Marion and brother, Guy. Her life changed dramatically when a young Airman, Fred swept her off her feet and the two became wed. Her home became the next base of assignment, places like: Dayton, Ohio; Little Rock, Arkansas; Ft. Worth, Tx; Fairbanks, Alaska; and San Antonio, Tx.

She and Fred were blessed with two children, Sandy and Randy. These children were fortunate to be continually showered with an uncommon love that shaped the rest of their lives. For these two, no matter the location, "Home" became a haven of rest and a shelter of protection. Betty's family continued to expand when she was blessed with a son-in-law, Bob, and daughter-in-law, Susie. Her joy continued to grow with the additions of her grandchildren; Coby, Blake, Amanda, and Chad. These four were continual recipients of Nana's love and were regularly treated with special snacks, surprise gifts, and as children, non-stop trips to Chuck E. Cheese.

Her church home was a source of strength and inspiration. She accepted Christ as an adult at the age of forty-one. Her love and devotion to Christ grew and matured throughout her years. In her thirty-five years in San Antonio, the Kirby Baptist Church became a place of worship, fellowship, service and encouragement. It was not uncommon to see "Aunt Betty" working in the nursery, preparing food in the kitchen, and other selfless acts of service.

Her short stay in a Houston Assisted Living home was but a step away from her permanent home, a heavenly home that was being prepared for her. There is great sadness for those who called her Betty, Aunt Betty, Betty Boop, mom, nana, and friend. However, there is also much joy in her home-going. She is being reacquainted with those who have preceded her on her journey- her parents, brother, husband, and various other loved ones. She is especially pleased to see and touch the Lord Who has guided her path for all of these years. Let us continue to grieve for our loss but let us also celebrate her joy and know that she is truly "home" at last."

A LOOK IN THE MIRROR

After spending time with family, Susie and I took a flight to Ft. Lauderdale and drove back to our apartment in Weston. We would return in time to worship at Oasis church, the church we had chosen to attend. Speaking of church, along with the new world at SOUTHCOM, my church experience had changed as well.

At church, I struggled with the following:

1. Pastoral identity. I was no longer the pastor of a church. For 22 years, I was "the pastor." When I walked into the church building or when parishioners saw me outside the church building, they knew that I was the pastor. Children would run up to me, hug me and say, "Good morning Pastor Randy!" Youth would no longer call me the affectionate name, "PR," short for "Pastor Randy." People did not ask me about my thoughts on the vision of the church. And so on... Personally, the feelings I experienced surprised me. Years prior, I would look at older, retired ministers who had been pastors and wondered why they seemed so miserable. I would find myself introducing myself to civilian ministers and saying something like, "I'm the Deputy Command Chaplain at SOUTHCOM...and I was a pastor for many years." I'm not sure why I added the "and I was a pastor" qualifier. I was having a hard time letting go of

that role. Understand, chaplains are ministers. They have a calling from God, are ordained, have an ecclesiastical endorsement, have advanced ministry degrees, and many years of ministry under their belt—not to mention specialized training. Few things rile a chaplain more than being asked, "when are you going back to the ministry?" Chaplains are ministers in unique environments—whether in the military, hospital, or other institution. But there is something special and dear about being a pastor of a local community and growing in faith together. More than anything, I missed the sense of community and being the spiritual leader.

2. Preaching. For 22 years I had prepared sermons for Sunday Morning, Sunday Night, and a devotion on Wednesday Night. I was mentally, physically, emotionally, and spiritually prepared to deliver a message that stayed true to the text and spoke to the needs of the congregation. In my "strategic" staff chaplain position, I had no Sunday responsibilities. So, when I went to church, I went to church and sat on a pew just like everyone else. Susie liked this because for the first time in 22 years, we were able to sit together. I soon discovered that, for me, it was much easier to preach a sermon than hear a sermon. I found myself thinking, "I'm not sure if I agree with that," or "I would have presented that a different way." I found myself like others whose mind would wander, even when great theological truths from the Word of God were being proclaimed!

3. Observations. I began to watch how things were presented in the church; the kind of language spoken, programs that were emphasized, and just the overall culture of the church. Before we settled on the church we attended, we visited other churches, which was also a new experience. Even though I had attended church as a youth, college student, and seminarian, and years as a

pastor, I was surprised at how awkward I felt in visiting. I didn't know anybody. They didn't know me. Some churches were extremely friendly, some not so much. We attended one church for a few weeks that was perfect. The preaching was perfect. The preacher's hair was perfect. The music was perfect. The modern facility was perfect. The programs were perfect. Even the somewhat affluent congregation was perfect. To tell you the truth, it kind of freaked me out! It was too glossy, too slick. Just my opinion, but the perfect aura of the church did not lend itself to a genuine faith walk. We didn't join, mainly because I felt like I was not perfect. Joining would have lowered the spiritual meter! In actuality, members of this church were not perfect either. They had times of stress and grief. They experienced doubt and perhaps despair. Their children and grandchildren were not always compliant and respectful. But, again from my perspective, transparency was not apparent. Certainly, a lesson learned for all of us—authenticity is key. Real Faith must be experienced with the presence of God and be practiced with a humble and vulnerable spirit. We decided to attend and join another congregation, one with deep theology and an openness of deeper and transparent relationships.

4. Accountability. There is an old joke about a man who woke up on a Sunday morning and told his wife, "I'm not going to church today." She replied, "why?" He said, "I'll give you three reasons. First, those people are just mean. Second, none of those people like me. Third, the music is too loud." She replied, "well, I can give you three reasons why you should go. First, you are a believer and should be in church on Sunday morning. Second, people depend on you to be there. And, third, most importantly, you are the pastor!" I have found that people expect their pastor to be in church most Sunday

mornings. What about when you are not the pastor? Aside from my wife, there wouldn't have been any family members asking me why I was skipping church. I don't have any real Sunday morning responsibilities. If I decide to go golfing or go to the beach, I seriously doubt if anyone from the church would call and check on me. For the first time in a long time, going to church was a choice. So what did we do most Sundays? We got up, got dressed and went to church. Why? It was not out of obligation. It was not out of some coercion. We went to church because intimacy with God is a priority. Singing songs of praise and hearing God's Word in a loving community is powerful and essential to spiritual development. Ministry is more than just outward observance. True ministry should flow from the inside out. As the expression says, "Ministry is an overflow of intimacy." When intimacy is not present, ministry will become an empty shell.

AWARD CEREMONIES

Public recognitions to military members is a long-standing tradition. While at SOUTHCOM, I either attended or provided the invocation for these ceremonies at the SOUTHCOM auditorium. One very unique ceremony occurred on 12 March 2009. This ceremony was not for one of our military members. It was for three civilians, but not employees at the SOUTHCOM Headquarters.

Marc Gonsalves, Keith Stansell, and Tom Howes were civilian contractors. They were crew members taking part in a routine mission to detect cocaine crops over southern Colombia on February 13, 2003. An in-flight emergency forced the pilot to crash land the aircraft. Revolutionary Armed Forces of Colombia (FARC) members stormed the crash site. The three were held in the jungles of Colombia for over five years.

After months of planning and cooperation with American Forces, Operation JACQUE commenced on 2 July 2008 to rescue the three contractors and 12 other hostages without firing a shot.

In one of the greatest military deceptions, Colombian soldiers posed as members of a fictitious non-government organization who had volunteered to fly the captives to meet one of the rebel leaders. The mission was designed to mimic previous hostage transfers, including the actual composition of the group and the type and markings of the helicopters used.[6]

The captives, who were unaware of the deception, were moved early on the morning of 2 July across the river to the landing zone where they were told by their captors that they were going to be moved to a different location. Two Mi-17 helicopters came to the landing area. One helicopter carried Colombian agents wearing Che Guevara T-shirts landed and picked up the hostages. In total, the helicopter spent 22 minutes on the ground, during which, the hostages were handcuffed and loaded aboard.

The local FARC commander, known as "Cesar" and an additional rebel boarded the helicopter along with the hostages. They were then persuaded to hand over their pistols before becoming airborne. In flight, they were subdued by Colombian forces. The hostages were still in the dark until they heard the words, in Spanish, "We are the national Army. You are free![7]

So, months later on 12 March 2009, these former hostages gathered in the comfort of the SOUTHCOM Headquarters to receive the Secretary of Defense Medal for the Defense of Freedom. The medal was developed by the Army's Institute of

Heraldry on September 27, 2001, to acknowledge civilian employees of the Department of Defense and contractors who were killed or wounded in the line of duty. At that point, only 37 individuals had been awarded this medal.

It was an honor to hear these men's story of survival and perseverance and was reminded of the sacrifice of those dedicated to the preservation of national security.

PARTNERSHIP

The SOUTHCOM motto was "Partnership of the Americas" This motto tied into the vision of SOUTHCOM: "We are a joint and interagency organization supporting U.S. national security interests, and with our partners, fostering security, stability, and prosperity in the Americas," which steers the mission: "we are ready to conduct joint and combined full-spectrum military operations and support whole-of-government efforts to enhance regional security and cooperation."[8] In brief, in my words, "we are all going to work together to make the world better, at least in the Americas."

The Command Chaplain's office was part of this unified team. Keeping in line with SOUTHCOM's vision and mission, we also used a "whole-of-government" approach, particularly among religious leadership to enhance regional security and cooperation.

One key strategy was gathering religious leaders with a tie to Partner-nation militaries to discuss cooperative efforts. In May 2009, our office hosted a Central America Regional Chaplain's Conference in Belize. Utilizing the expertise of the SOUTHCOM State Partnership Program Coordinator, we joined hands with the

U.S. National Guard State Partnership Program (SPP). Established in 1993, the program links U.S. States with partner countries for the purpose of supporting the security cooperation objectives of the Combatant Commander. States form a partnership with individual nations. The State Partners actively participate in several engagement activities utilizing the unique civil-military nature of the National Guard to interact with military forces of foreign countries. During the conference in Belize, State National Guard chaplains from states participating in the SPP in these regions were matched with military chaplains/religious representatives from the same regions with the purpose of extending dialogue, building relationships, and sharing resource information.

Along with the Chaplain's Office and the State Partnership Program, the third "leg" of the engagement was the use of the Public/Private Cooperation (PPC) Directorate at SOUTHCOM. The program seeks to build noncommercial partnerships with public agencies and private sectors to build collaboration. Faith-based organizations have tremendous resources and manpower that can assist areas affected by a disaster.

Some guidelines are:

1. It is an interaction between a DoD component and a private entity.
2. It is voluntary, not mandated or part of an organizational framework. There is no financial payment or contract.
3. The bywords are "mutual" and "shared;" this would include mutually agreed goals and governance, and shared decision-making.
4. Private sector includes not only corporations, but also Non-Governmental Organizations (NGOs), universities,

foundations, community-based and other private sector organizations; almost any kind of entity other than the UN or another country.

5. Other federal agencies may also be involved, although normally in conjunction with a private sector entity.9

Faith communities, including churches, have a desire to help during tragedies. Building these partnerships before tragedy strikes builds and strengthens communication and collaboration.

There were some things I learned from the Initial Regional Chaplain's Conference:

1. Never refer to the United States as "America." For most of us Americans, when we think of "America," we think of the United States. Partner nations in Central America and South America will quickly point out that "America" is a much broader, geographical term.

2. Partnerships create a lot of synergy. Different organizations and different nations cooperating together provide unique perspectives. "Partnership of the Americas" was more than just a motto, it was a focus that could be leveraged to provide life-giving assistance.

3. North Americans do not have a monopoly on Christianity. People in other nations love Jesus too. Of course, I knew this, but seeing and hearing these religious leaders reminded me of the richness of faith in our world. The vast majority of these religious leaders were Roman Catholic.

4. Every nation in the SOUTHCOM AOR has a unique history, traditions, and customs. Belize is no exception. The Mayan civilization spread into the area of Belize between 1500 BC and AD 300. Ruins are still present. We had the opportunity to tour them during the conference. Belize is often considered a Caribbean country in Central America because it has a history

similar to English-speaking Caribbean nations. Belize's institutions and official language reflect its history as a British colony.

During my time at SOUTHCOM, our office also hosted these types of Religious Engagements with Partner Nations in Montego Bay, Jamaica and at the SOUTHCOM Conference Facility in Doral.

One significant event in Belize occurred during the second night of the conference. We were all housed in one hotel in Belize City. In the middle of the night, my bed began to shake. I woke up and realized my whole room was shaking. After my head cleared, I realized it was an earthquake. Though I was familiar what to do in the event of a fire, tornado, or hurricane, I did not know how to respond to an earthquake. My gut reaction was to hide under the bed. I rolled over to the floor and attempted to scoot under the bed, but it was blocked by a wooden frame. I hunkered down in that area between the bed and the nightstand, what seemed like several minutes, but in reality, was only a few seconds. After it was over, all seemed well. I didn't hear any commotion in the hall, so I just went back to sleep. I learned the next morning that the earthquake had occurred off the coast of Guatemala, and Belize felt part of the rumbling. I also learned later that my position beside the bed and the nightstand was optimal. Experts advise not to be under the bed in case the roof falls and the bed collapses on top of you. The best strategy was to find a "triangle." Find a place that if the roof collapses, you have a better chance at survival if your triangle holds. So, my placement beside and not under that bed was my unintentional triangle.

The next morning, over breakfast, our group would laugh about being in an earthquake. The events in early January 2010 would be a chilling reminder of what could have been.

Operation UNIFIED RESPONSE

On 12 Jan 2010, the strongest earthquake in Haiti in more than 200 years, measuring 7.0 on the Richter scale, struck the impoverished Caribbean nation. The earthquake's epicenter was south-west of Haiti's capital, Port-au-Prince, which suffered extensive damage.

The nearby cities of Carrefour and Jacmel and other areas to the west and south of Port-au-Prince were also affected, with the town of Léogâne 80% destroyed. Over 220,000 were killed and over 300,000 were injured. Over 3 million people required humanitarian assistance of some kind. The president of Haiti, Rene Garcia Preval, declared a national state of emergency and requested assistance from the United States and other members of the international community.

Once this help was requested, SOUTHCOM was on alert. Operation UNIFIED RESPONSE began. Immediately, the SOUTHCOM Standing Joint Force Headquarters (SJFH) was activated. SJFH is composed of men and women of various expertise, mainly operational planners and command and control specialists, to deploy in situations like this. They are a type of First Responders, heading straight to the scene, immediately assessing the situation and making recommendations to the SOUTHCOM Commander.

A joint task force was formed—JTF-Haiti. Several teams,

including a Chaplain Corps team was deployed. In the coming weeks, several different military personnel would follow to provide logistical assistance to the relief efforts. The "battle rhythm" at the SOUTHCOM headquarters had changed. Offices were required to be manned 24/7. In order to augment HQ forces, NORTHCOM personnel based out of Colorado Springs, CO, provided additional manpower, including the Chaplain's office. We were placed on 12-hour shifts.

In order to fulfill our role, we had a three-fold purpose:

1. Provide continual support and communication to the JTF-Haiti Command Chaplain. His responsibility was to maintain command and control over all Chaplain Corps members in country. We would provide any support needed in order for mission requirements to be met.
2. Assist in linking Humanitarian Assistance relief needed with Faith-community assets including faith groups and faith-based Non-Governmental Organizations.This experience was a real eye-opener to the incredible resources that were available, cooperation across religious/philosophical/cultural lines, and perspective on faith-community involvement. Most impressive was observing the ways disasters bring out the best in people. I have noticed this fact throughout my life as a pastor and chaplain. Whether it involves a neighbor experiencing an accident, illness, or death, it is common for the local community to gather and offer assistance. Living in the Houston, TX, area, damages from Tropical Storms and Hurricanes would occur. When they did, the community became galvanized in their assistance in some remarkable ways. It didn't matter if the neighbor was Christian or non-Christian, Republican or

Democrat, Northerner or Southerner, even if the neighbor was a Philadelphia Eagles fan(!), help would quickly arrive. When international disasters occurred, the same compassion and help materialized. The only difference was the scope and resources available.

3. Provide Pastoral Care.

When the earthquake occurred, SOUTHCOM had a team in team of military members in Port-a-Prince. Unfortunately, we lost a military member of the SOUTHCOM team when a hotel collapsed. We were able to provide pastoral care to his widow. In addition, as the days went by, family members of the members of the SJFH became concerned at the length of the deployment. We reached out to them, gathering them together for question-and-answer sessions. Members of the SJFH were doing well, but the stress was great. Though bullets were not flying, and they had relatively safe conditions, they did not experience "Combat Stress," however, they did experience "Operational Stress."

Operational Stress had an impact on SOUTHCOM HQ personnel as well. The strain was felt physically, mentally, emotionally, and spiritually. Chaplains are not immune to this stress. One example of this, that my wife loves to remind me, is when I was back at home in our apartment in Weston. I was taking an uncommon day off. I was sitting on my porch surrounded by a little screened-in patio that overlooked a pond. The pond also attracted ducks. Being a bit tired and stressed (yes, this is my excuse), I looked out the screen enclosure. I noticed small ducklings were falling out of the wings of a mother duck. I yelled to Susie, "come quick, this duck is having babies!" She came, looked at the ducks, looked at me and replied dryly, "You know, Randy, a duck is a bird. Birds lay eggs." I looked again and said with disappointment, "Oh yeah." I believe I took a nap shortly after!

The response and extended hours lasted six weeks at SOUTHCOM HQ. In early March, schedules returned to normal.

On 1 March, members of SOUTHCOM's Standing Joint Force Headquarters returned. This small response team had experienced the difficult and sometimes horrifying ground-level response. They had left family and friends to respond to this humanitarian crisis. In speaking with them, they made some observations:

1. The quietness of the SOUTHCOM Headquarters was striking. The camps were in constant noise with the sound of gas generators.
2. In Haiti, showers were minimal/non-existent the first two weeks.
3. Mosquitos were ubiquitous. Double mosquito netting was utilized.
4. One person noted that in the 40 days he was in Haiti, he only saw three birds—one seagull and two crows. He attributed it to deforestation and tarantulas.
5. No cats, some rats.
6. There was a concern for malaria. Members took malaria pills thirty days after returning.
7. All were definitely glad to be back.

The response of USSOUTHCOM, JTF-Haiti military members, United Nations, Partner Nations, Helping agencies, and Non-governmental agencies, including Faith-Based organizations was impressive.

In a report in 2010 I wrote these words:

"In today's military vernacular, "resiliency" is a

common term. The word comes from the Latin "resiliens," to rebound or recoil. It is defined as the power to return to an original form after being twisted, compressed or stretched. The Haitian people have seen their country and their lives twisted, compressed and stretched. With the help of the international community and the realization of their own abilities, they will continue to strive toward that goal.

Faith-based NGOs will continue to maintain an active presence in Haiti. They possess the human, physical, technical, and financial resources needed to support and implement small- and large-scale initiatives. They will continue to do extraordinary things in the lives of the Haitian people. In future foreign Humanitarian Assistance/Disaster Relief (HA/DR) operations, military chaplains, with their unique ecclesiastical ties and military training will continue to maintain a presence that will influence both the military and civilian organizations during humanitarian crises. Military chaplains should continue to strive to develop a culture of preparedness. They should be properly trained in order enhance the chaplain's effectiveness as a as liaison for the commander to faith-based NGOs operating in the Joint Operational Area (JOA.) A joint-doctrinal awareness, the provision of practical training, and continued dialogue would highlight and elevate the role of military chaplains as they immerse themselves in a humanitarian unity of effort."

More information of Operation UNIFIED RESPONSE is found in Flight Notes #4.

GOLF

The month of March brought the game of golf to Doral. As mentioned, the SOUTHCOM Headquarters was located across the street from the Doral Country Club. This course had a rich history with the PGA tour. The Doral Open was held at the club from 1962 to 2006. During that span it was typically considered one of the premiere non-major tournaments on tour. Since then, it underwent various name changes, but continued to host PGA tournaments until 2016. So, during my time at SOUTHCOM, every Spring brought the excitement of the PGA Tour to South Florida. In an effort to be good neighbors, SOUTHCOM leadership allowed personnel to volunteer during the tournament. A tournament of this type involves a massive number of volunteers. Perks for volunteers included a T-shirt, the ability to have a close-up view of the players, and the opportunity to play the course, at a future date. I volunteered in two of these tournaments. In both, I was an "Advance Marshal" (Obviously, with my name, it was a perfect fit!) Every hole had "Marshals" to help direct the crowd and hold the "quiet please" signs. The Advance Marshal was assigned a pro golf two-some and actually followed those players from hole-to-hole. The advantage of being the Advance Marshal was the ability to see and experience the entire course and not be limited to one hole. The other advantage is that Advance Marshals were assigned to high-profile players. One memorable twosome was serving in this role with two giants on the tour—Tiger Woods and Phil Mickelson. Seeing them up close gave a greater appreciation of their personality and interaction with the crowd. One was very intense and businesslike, the other more relaxed and collegial. The most impressive site was their incredibly smooth swing and impact on the ball.

Weeks later, I was able to play the course. They must have lengthened it because it would take at least two, if not three shots to get to their one drive! There was a silver lining in my realization that my abilities were far below a pro golfer—that is, I would never be tempted to quit the ministry to go on tour! Hey, we all have gifts! Though Tiger and Phil can read a green and make the shot, they probably can't exegete a Biblical text and deliver a sermon!

STAN, STAN, AND BORIS

Another golf story. Near my home in Weston, there was a public golf course. When I had the chance, I would play. One of the frustrating things about South Florida was the changing weather. Many days, I would look out my office window and see the sun shining and a gentle breeze blowing. On days I had planned to play golf that afternoon, it was great to know that the weather would be perfect. Many times, it was perfect…while I was in the office. The problem was, by the time I was able to get on the course, the weather had changed. The sun was creating warm air temperatures adding to the moisture and sea breezes which then brought showers and thunderstorms. The good news was that the showers were normally short-lived.

One day, I arrived at the course. The weather was ideal. When I walked into the club house, I told the man behind the desk that I did not have a tee time and that I was a single (meaning I was the only one playing.) Oftentimes a single will be paired with another twosome or threesome. That was the case today. I was paired with three men who introduced themselves as Stan, Stan, and Boris. They told me they were on vacation from Canada. Stan and Stan were dressed very similarly and seemed to have a very close relationship. They rode in one golf cart. Boris and I rode in the second cart.

Between the four of us, conversation mainly centered around golf. On the third hole, Boris asked me what I did for a living. I told him that I was a chaplain in the Air Force. Allow me to pause at this point in the story. In my Air Force experiences at Lackland and Randolph, it was very common for me to spend a late afternoon or two on the golf course during my annual tour. Sometimes I would be able to get on the course and play alone—which to some sounds very boring. For me, especially after spending the day with a lot of people, having some time alone was great. Most days, I would be paired up with one or two or three others that I did not know. Invariably, around the third hole, the question would be asked of me, "So what do you do?"

My reply would be, "I'm a chaplain."

Many times, that response would cause eyes to widen followed by a furrowed brow, with the response, "You could have told me that sooner!" In the pause immediately after saying those words, I could see the man retracing his steps and rewinding the mental tape, thinking about all the inappropriate comments he had made and the language that spewed from his mouth after an unfortunate shot. I guess he figured that ministers should not hear those kinds of things! I always felt bad because many times, the quality of their game seemed to diminish after this revelation. When the subsequent golf shots were wayward, my playing partners tended to hold back, mutter under their breath or just say, "shucks" or "darn" or a slow, "dag-nabbit!"

So, on the third hole, I told Boris that I was a chaplain. Instead of showing a surprised-dread look, he was genuinely interested and asked me questions about where I worked and what it was like to be a chaplain. When I asked about his work, he just said he was a retired government worker. The weather held up, the golf was fun, and the conversation between shots continued. With Stan and Stan in one cart, and Boris in the other with me, we were having a great time.

Driving down the 18th fairway, he dropped some surprising information. With a wry smile, he said, "I didn't mention it, but I am a retired Soviet Tank commander." Yes, he was a retired government worker of the former Soviet Union! Similar to the way everyday Americans look at me when I mention I am a minister, I stared right at and through him.

I immediately replayed my conversation with him in the past four hours evaluating if I gave any information that would violate my Top-Secret Clearance. When I felt I was in the clear, my response was a weak, "Oh, that's interesting." It was only at that point it occurred to me that "Boris" was not a typical Canadian name!

So, we finished our round. Stan, Stan, and Boris went on their way. I walked to my car wondering if I needed to report this encounter with the security manager. I imagined the report he would make, "SOUTHCOM Deputy Command Chaplain had social interaction with former Soviet operative. Upon investigation, no classified information was leaked; however, he displayed a lack of situational awareness by being distracted in perfecting his backswing and follow-through."

PASSING OF A FRIEND

One September afternoon in 2010, I was informed that my friend and fellow chaplain, Charlie Bolin, while on a tour of duty at Andrews AFB, Maryland, suffered a heart attack and died. His death was a great loss for me personally and for the Air Force Reserve Chaplain Corps. Many outpoured their love and support, especially those he served. On the Funeral Home website, family and friends were invited to share memories and condolences. The comments were a tribute to him and reflected the impact of his civilian and military chaplain ministry.

One comment read, "Chaplain Charlie was a very wonderful and unique person. He was definitely God's servant, and I am a better person for having him placed in my path of life. Our worship team, 'Sounds of New Hope,' shared our music at the 10:00a.m. service at the Riviera Hotel for about 5 years. During that time, we were involved in the most unique ministry that we ever saw. Charlie was a wonderful, bright candle in the middle of a really dark place. He showed us patience, love, happiness, tolerance, understanding and stability. God Bless You, Charlie! You are part of His family in heaven, and we thank you for allowing us to be part of your life. Another read, "It was an honor to know and serve with Chaplain, Col Bolin during several Patriot Defenders. He will be greatly missed by all the members of the 610th SFS. My heartfelt condolences to Chaplain Bolin's family."[9]

These messages were a tribute to Ch Bolin. They are also examples of words of tribute for all military ministers who are "Citizen Airmen"—men and women who minister in civilian faith communities as well as military environments. The impact of these men and women is significant in the communities they serve—in both civilian and military capacities.

Ch Bolin proudly served in his own unique way as a hotel chaplain on the Las Vegas strip and a military chaplain dedicated to training young chaplains and chaplain assistants. He is part of the legacy of men and women who carry the proud tradition of Citizen Airmen serving in the Chaplain Corps.

He was well-loved and will be missed.

ANOTHER OUT OF OFFICE CONVERSATION

One thing that I am certain…my wife did not marry me for my car. Years prior, when we were married, my wedding jitters were not that I would somehow mess up my vows, drop the ring, or step on her dress. My most pressing concern was that after the reception, after the rice (actually bird seed) throwing, after getting settled in my ten-year-old Mercury Comet, and after turning the key that it would fail to start.

I could just imagine everyone standing around waving goodbye, sending the couple off for their new life together. Having to ask for a jump or banging on the starter would not have boded well for the nuptials. Fortunately, that crisis was averted; however, for most of our married life, owning older cars with ubiquitous starting problems was common. So, when I came out of the Olive Garden restaurant with a take-out order, I was frustrated but not totally surprised that my Chevy Malibu would not start. By the way, I have no brand loyalty. I have owned Fords, Chevys, Toyotas, a Mercury, and an Acura. My only desire is functionality utilizing good stewardship (spiritual talk for cheap).

So, I called my insurance company. They provided an emergency road service and after a thirty-minute wait, the tow truck arrived. A wiry, 30ish man got out of the truck and began to negotiate the best way to load the car onto the truck. In the process, he noticed the Department of Defense sticker on my windshield. His eyes lit up and said that he spent four years in the Army. I told him that I was in the Air Force and was currently stationed at SOUTHCOM in Miami. Once in the truck, he in the driver's seat, me in the passenger seat, we made our 25-minute drive to the garage of my choice.

On the way, he commenced to tell me about his military life—he reminisced about his assignments, his experiences, and the number of women that he met along the way. He bragged about his sexual exploits while using some colorful non-church language. I just listened. As we were a few minutes away from our destination, he said to me…"I have picked up a lot of people that have broken down like this, but you have a calmness about yourself." I finally interjected, it may be partly what I do for the Air Force, I'm a chaplain." For the first time in twenty minutes there was complete silence. His hands were ten and two on the steering wheel, looking straight ahead. He then slowly turned to me with one eye on the road and one eye on me and said the words I have heard on the golf course, "You could have told me that 20 minutes ago." I laughed and told him that he didn't ask! I went on to tell him that beyond being a chaplain, I was a believer—that any calmness that I had was because of a personal relationship with Jesus Christ. Through a simple conversation, the tow truck experience turned into a divine appointment that allowed the presentation of the Gospel.

Please don't ask me if God caused my car not to start so that I could have the opportunity to have this conversation. I don't need to dissect the manner in which God works. As they say in the military, these types of things are "above my pay grade." I do know however, that God is constantly at work in places and circumstances that I least expect. I am sure there have been some opportunities along the way that I have blown because my countenance was not as calm as on that day. So, I encourage you to take look at your car that needs service, your house that needs repairs, your body that needs a checkup, and countless other challenges that we face as an opportunity to share our faith, even in the midst of adversities.

PANAMAX

SOUTHCOM participated and hosted several military exercises. One of the most prominent was PANAMAX. PANAMAX is a U.S.-sponsored, multinational annual exercise that provides an opportunity to conduct security and stability operations, practice interoperability with our partners, and build upon capability to plan and execute complex multinational operations.[11]

At the time, the majority of the exercise was in the country of Panama. Several directorates from SOUTHCOM would travel in-country. One of my main responsibilities was planning for contingencies involving Joint Chaplain Corps personnel. So, I was given the opportunity to travel for this two-week tour. "Planning" and "military" go hand in hand. The military is continually planning for the "what if." Exercises help test capabilities and hopefully identify deficiencies before the actual event.

The SOUTHCOM website states, "The focus of PANAMAX is to exercise a variety of responses to a request for assistance from the government of Panama to protect and guarantee safe passage of traffic through the Panama Canal, ensure its neutrality, and respect national sovereignty. This exercise is designed to execute stability operations under the auspices of United Nations Security Council Resolutions; provide interoperability training for the participating multinational staffs; and build participating nation capability to plan and execute complex multinational operations. PANAMAX provides opportunities for the participating nations to join efforts to counter threats posed by violent and dangerous groups, provide humanitarian relief as necessary, and maintain free and unfettered access to the Panama Canal."[12]

The Command Center for the exercise was located in a Panama hotel in a large area with numerous tables with a computer on each. Exercise scenarios that had been developed over the past few months were ready to be launched. It provided a response across the Command and avoided a "stovepipe" approach to meeting the challenges.

The chaplain table happened to be alongside a 40ish civilian that worked logistics. We would be working shoulder to shoulder for the next two weeks. He confessed that he had never really been around a chaplain, and I don't think he was initially excited about the arrangement. In the days that followed, he opened up. He told me that he was an atheist. When he revealed this fact, he stopped to evaluate my reaction. With my best poker face, I said, "O.K!"

He asked, "Why do we need church? Why can't we just live our lives without being condemned?" In talking more with him, it was apparent that he had been exposed to a *hammer-down* religious background that heaped tons of condemnations.

I mentioned that in the Scripture, Jesus was harsher with the religious crowd than he was with those who struggled with sin. I admitted that some churches forget this. Later in the week, he mentioned that he was dating a girl back in Miami who was Catholic. Though he was not a believer, he was attending weekly Mass with her. He said he was learning some things and was open to what was being said. My prayer was that our two-week working relationship softened some preconceived notions on chaplains and religion. Throughout the exercise, I had the opportunity to speak with others—some I knew from the Headquarters, and some I had recently met. "Divine Appointments," those that God seemed to orchestrate were plentiful.

COMMUNITY

A few months later, I ran into the young logistician at a Miami restaurant. He seemed genuinely glad to see me. I asked him if he was still dating the girl. He said no, and then volunteered that he was still going to Mass. I was a bit perplexed and I blurted out, "Why?" After gaining my composure, I more calmly asked, "So are you still an atheist?"

He answered, "yes."

I replied, "I guess I got the impression you were attending Mass just to impress your girlfriend."

He said, "I was, but after we broke up, I kind of missed the feel of being part of a community." I continued to pray for him as he went his way.

This interaction both encouraged and discouraged me. It was encouraging that he was still a part of a Christian community and that perhaps some of the teachings would rub off. It was discouraging because his focus was on community and community alone. Outwardly, there was no desire for spiritual awareness or growth, no indication that he was wanting to experience true faith, and no openness to a deeper, Godly relationship. He simply enjoyed the fellowship and camaraderie among the membership. My sense of discouragement was not only for him, but for our church families. How many people in our churches have this same mentality? Though fellowship or community is an important quality in our churches, it should never be an end to itself. Christian community must always have a faith foundation with a focus on the mission of Christ and the church community.

As 1 John 1:3-4 states, "We proclaim to you what we have seen and heard, so that you also may have fellowship with us. And our fellowship is with the Father and with his Son, Jesus Christ. We write this to make our joy complete."

Yes, complete joy comes through a relationship with Jesus Christ. May our fellowship always be wrapped in His presence.

I'M TALKING TO MY FRIEND!

I was scheduled to take a military trip to Norfolk VA. Since we lived closer to Ft. Lauderdale and the airport wasn't as busy as Miami, I boarded a plane at the Ft. Lauderdale airport. I took my seat. Shortly after, a middle-aged woman with somewhat wild blond hair sat next to me. She wanted to have a conversation. Normally, I would welcome this. I have experienced some "Divine

Appointments" where I believe God allowed me to interact with people and maybe provide some pastoral advice, guidance, etc…As this woman talked, it was evident that she had visited one of the airport bars before her flight.

She asked me the inevitable question, "So what do you do for a living?" I was tempted to say that I was in sales of an international redemptive society and that the benefits were out of this world! Instead, I simply said, "I am a military chaplain." Her eyes lit up. She said, "Really! That is wonderful, I really respect that. I am an atheist." She leaned in a little closer, uncomfortably closer, "But I am a nice atheist. I am not like some of those (expletive) atheists that make a big deal about faith and God. Let people live their own lives…" And she went on and on and became louder and louder. What began as a quiet, personal, civilized conversation became a rant. Finally, a lady sitting across the aisle, one row up leaned over and pleaded, "could you please keep your voice down?" This simply elevated the volume until the inebriated woman said, "Excuse me, but I am talking to my friend!" Unfortunately, she was talking about me.

I gave a subtle shake of the head to the woman in front of us, as if I was in a hostage situation—which in many ways I was—indicating that I was not a friend. At this point, I realized that drastic actions were necessary. I gave out a big yawn and said to my new "friend," I think I'm going to take a little nap. She seemed to understand, calmed down, and started reading a book. At one point, I looked out the corner of my eye and saw that she had fallen asleep. When she awoke, she seemed to have a more positive disposition.

I'm not sure if I shirked my responsibility that day to have any kind of impact in this woman's life. It was an uncomfortable conversation but was good to meet another nice atheist. Hopefully, another believer was able to converse with her. I hope and pray that one day, we run into each other on the streets of heaven as she tells me the rest of her story.

BE NICE!

Even though I am a Christian and a minister, I have my days. When I am a little testy, my wife is known to say to me, "be nice." In our rough and tumble world, the reminder to "be nice" is worthy. One day I was making one of my regular trips to Publix—a grocery store chain in Florida. I managed to fill my basket with necessary items and hit the supermarket jackpot of not having to wait in line. As I placed my items on the conveyer belt, the middle-age female checker began scanning and pushing the items down to a younger male employee to bag. As I placed, she scanned, and he bagged, I heard her say to her young counterpart, "I'm always nice to customers; you never know when they are going to come back and shoot the place up. If they do, I want them to remember that I was nice and maybe spare me."

When she said these words, two things came to mind. First, how sad it is that we live in a society where having a person come and "shoot the place up" is even something to seriously consider. Second, I was trying to wrap my mind around the fact that the only reason why she was nice to people is so she could potentially survive a shooting spree. As I finished placing items on the conveyer, my eyes met hers. Being a regular customer at Publix I felt that I had some familiarity with many of the employees. This woman had scanned my groceries before, and indeed she was always nice. Being nice is a good thing. I really can't argue with being nice. But I wonder about our motivations. As believers, are we nice to others because it is an overflow of the joy of Christ in our lives? Are we nice because we have a peace that passes all understanding and God has placed calmness in our otherwise restless hearts?

As a believer, hopefully, fundamentally the answer is "yes." However, all of us must be careful of those other dark motivations. Are we only nice to our boss, supervisor, and chairman of the finance committee because they directly affect our future? Are we just as nice to the low-profile janitor who cleans our toilets as the commander or wealthy businessman who yields great influence? Do we make friends and build key alliances (like on the T.V. show "Survivor") simply to get another step closer to the top? We need to be honest about our niceness quotient. We may chuckle at the conversation with the checker and her seemingly warped view of niceness, but it was a reminder that I need to look beyond, at my motivations of niceness.

If we truly love the Lord with all our heart and love others beyond ourselves then our niceness will be genuinely consistent no matter the circumstance. Admittedly, as our old nature and new nature clash, when we come in contact with people that rub us the wrong way, and when we find ourselves in seasons of life that don't lend to positive feelings, niceness can be a struggle. As in all areas of our Christian life, we can lean on the transformational power of God's Word and his abiding presence to show us the way.

To close the loop in my supermarket encounter, after our eyes met, and she finished scanning my cantaloupe and eggs, I entered into a brief conversation with the checker. We spoke about the world we live and its uncertainty and engaged in some friendly banter. I must confess, as I gathered my bags, I said something that was intended to lighten the conversation. (Fortunately, I was not in my military uniform.) I told her, "Don't worry about me, if I ever come here and cause any trouble, I'll remember you, because you were nice." I waited for her laugh, but it never came—she backed away slightly and muttered "O.K...". I gingerly walked out the door wondering if she was going to call Homeland Security. I went home and told my wife the story. She just looked at me. She didn't have to say the words, I knew what she was thinking. Be nice.

MISSING TEXAS

At SOUTHCOM, I was assigned a government cell phone (Blackberry.) They were designed for government business. We would use them for telephone calls and checking news reports. Sometimes sports news would appear. Being from Texas, I was interested in Texas-based sports. I would particularly follow the scores of the Dallas Cowboys, the San Antonio Spurs, and the Texas A&M Aggies.

One day, in looking at scores, I saw a school with the first two letter, "UT" ending in the prefix "AH." I felt like I was familiar with the University of Texas University system and their locations. I knew of the flagship University of Texas in Austin (UT), as well as the University of Texas at Arlington (UTA), University of Texas at San Antonio (UTSA), University of Texas at El Paso (UTEP) and University in Texas at Dallas (UTD.) What I could not figure out was the location of University of Texas…AH. UT-AH. Then it occurred to me, the school was "UTAH!"

At this point, I could not blame being sleep-deprived, I was simply misguided and perhaps a bit homesick.

THE PASTORAL CHAPLAIN

Though my primary duties were "strategic," because of my visibility with members during planning meetings, staff meetings, military exercises and the prominent cross on the left side of my chest, pastoral interactions were common. Some were in the workplace where someone would take me aside and say, "chaplain, I have a question for you…" Sometimes the counseling would be more formal and would entail an office counseling. I conducted funerals. I served on death notification teams. A death notification team is composed of two members, a military officer and a chaplain. Through the Red Cross and various military processes, there is a requirement for a family member to be personally notified in the event of the death of a Servicemember. Of the half-dozen notifications I was a part, half of those notified at their homes were already aware, our announcement was a formality. The other three were complete surprises. Imagine the grief of opening your front door and seeing two military officers in their Service Dress Uniforms. When you realize one of them is a chaplain, you know it will be devastating news. The words, "we regret to inform you…" bring anguish and pain. On one occasion, it brought a woman to her knees, sobbing loudly. These notifications are emotionally excruciating for the family member. They also have an effect on the ones delivering the message.

On a lighter note, I was also able to conduct weddings. One day, I was approached by one of our SOUTHCOM civilians, a woman in her late 30s, asking if I would be willing to officiate her wedding. I told her I would love to officiate and that I required two counseling sessions prior to the wedding ceremony. She agreed. Her fiancée lived in California and was planning to come to Miami in the coming weeks. We set an appointment in my office. On the day of the counseling the two of them arrived in civilian clothes. I knew that he was a military member, in the Navy, stationed in California, but I didn't know much more. In talking with the couple, I asked them what their plans would be after the wedding since he lived in California, and she lived in Miami. His answer stunned me. He said, "I may retire, it depends if I get my second star." This man was a Navy Admiral! I sat a bit straighter and said, "Sir, I wasn't aware of that!

Months later, the wedding was conducted on a beach overlooking the Atlantic Ocean. I was dressed in my dress blues, the Admiral was in his Navy uniform, the bride was dressed in white. The wedding was beautiful, and the background was stunning...well mostly. Since the beach was a public beach, a crowd of beachgoers were lingering behind me to be a part of the experience. I did not see the wedding pictures, but I am fairly certain they included random men in speedos and women in skimpy bikinis!

JTF-BRAVO

In March 2011 I traveled to JTF (Joint Task Force)—Bravo, a deployed location in Honduras. I went to make a "Command

Chaplain Engagement" to check on the Chaplain Corps team and build relations with the JTF-Bravo leadership. In addition, I was asked to be the speaker for the annual National Day of Prayer Luncheon.

On this trip, I faced the known and the unknown. I knew the mission and purpose of this group. This Joint Task force operated out of Soto Cano Air Base, a Honduran military installation. It is comprised of both Honduran civilians and U.S. military personnel—total base population was around 1000. The location was a central base of operations to foster security and stability to the region.

What I did not know when I boarded the flight in Miami what was to come in Tegucigalpa, the capital city of Honduras. The Tegucigalpa Toncontin Airport is ranked the second most dangerous runway in the world. Pilots are forced to negotiate the mountainous terrain to land on a runway measuring less than 7,000 feet long. I sat on the left side of the aircraft, by the window when the pilot made an abrupt left bank to enter the runway. I literally saw clothes hanging on a line and if the window had been open, I was convinced I could have touched them. Just when it seemed like we were about to spin out of control, the pilot leveled out, seemingly just in time to enter the runway. Upon landing, the passengers broke out in cheers—a practice I have heard is commonplace.

After a long, bumpy bus ride to the base, I finally arrived. Across the base, spirits seemed to be high, and the Chaplain team was fully engaged. The next day, I gave my talk at the Prayer Breakfast. I spoke on the story of Noah and the leaf of promise. My desire was to give a word of hope and encouragement to these men and women, far from home and family, as they fulfilled their mission in this deployed setting. These are some of the thoughts spoken on that day:

"Remember the story of Noah? The account of this ancient mariner is well-known. Most of us can recount the beginning of the story—Noah is commissioned to build an ark and gather the animals. We also know the end of the story—the ark settles on the top of a mountain and God sends a rainbow.

What most cannot recite however, is the middle of the story, the time between the obedient decision to build the ark and the completion of the mission. Both in Noah's life adventure, and our own, we must be careful not to race to the rainbow and miss life "in the meantime."

When Noah, his wife, three sons and three daughters-in-law shut the door of the massive floating menagerie, they were not sure what the future held. Genesis 6 gives a very detailed account of God's ark building specifications, animal logistics movement and ration procurement. Finally, when everything was in place and God gave the word, the door of the floating barge was closed. The flurry of activity was don, the rain was falling, the water was rising. Without any navigation system, all Noah could do was hold on and wait.

One detail you may not remember about this account is that though it rained for 40 days and 40 nights, Noah was stuck in the dark recesses of the 45-foot high, three deck structure for one year and seventeen days. Poor Noah didn't have a clue about the length of his assignment. He simply observed and waited for his next order. We all stand in the sandals of Noah. As the old saying goes, "We don't know what the future holds but we know Who holds the future." In our own deployments, we can meticulously prepare, work hard and look forward to the rainbow of completion. Ultimately, however we simply live in the meantime attempting to remain faithful, even when we experience frustration, darkness, and an occasional stink.

A key verse in the account is in Genesis 8:1, "But God remembered Noah..." Though Noah may have felt forsaken, in reality, he was never forgotten. At the right time, God caused a wind to pass upon the earth. The water began to recede. Not knowing the condition of the earth outside, Noah eventually sent out a dove who returned with a freshly picked olive leaf. That may not sound like much, but it was front-page news for Noah. The end of the journey was near. Soon, he would experience the joy of the rainbow with his feet upon dry ground. In the meantime, however he clutched the leaf with its corresponding promise.

Today, a leaf of hope can come through a scripture verse, a phrase of a song, an encouraging word and a number of other ways. Make a point this week to recognize some personal God-leafs. While you are at it, share them with others—we need all the help we can get while we live in the meantime.

Later that night, a young army female lieutenant gave me a copy of a letter she had sent to her family:

"Dear Mom, Grandma, and Maria,
I know that sometimes I get wrapped up in my busy life and am not always the best granddaughter, daughter or friend. So I wanted to write a quick letter to the women in my life that are the most important and let you know that I love you.

Today we had a National Prayer Luncheon on base and the chaplain who spoke was very sincere and motivational. He told us a story about Noah and the Ark.

In the story, a dove was sent out every day to find something good. One day it came back with a leaf and it gave hope that there was still life. It was amazing that something so simple gave hope. It was a reminder for me that often I expect bigger things and I am always so worried about work and life that I don't stop to appreciate what I have already been given. I am overall healthy and when I am sick I have healthcare. In a world with such economic problems I have a wonderful career. I have been afforded the opportunity for education and travel. Most importantly I have family and friends who love me no matter what I do or what happens and for that I am truly grateful.

During the chaplain's speech he told us we should share our hope with others and let them know we care. So, I am enclosing a copy of the Prayer Luncheon Program with a leaf that came off the flower arrangement that was utilized during Lunch. (The chaplain said it was okay. I promise I didn't make off with the leaves.)

When the leaf finally gets to you I hope it makes you smile and brings you a day filled with hope!"

The event went well. The local commander surprised me with the presentation of a large wooden Chaplain Corps seal that was made by a Honduran craftsman. On the back is written, "This Chaplain Corps Seal is presented to Ch, Lt Col Randy Marshall on the occasion of the 2011 National Prayer Luncheon, Soto Cano Air Base, Honduras. Many thanks for the sharing of your ministry gifts. From the men and women of Joint Task Force-Bravo and Army Support Activity." The gift was much appreciated, but it was large, some two feet in diameter. I was hoping it wouldn't weigh down my flight in the aircraft back home as it attempted to negotiate the mountains surrounding Tegucigalpa!

BUILDING CAPACITY

In October 31, 2011, the SOUTHCOM Command Chaplain's office hosted a Florida Religious Leaders Conference. The conference provided a forum to enhance communications and collaboration of military chaplain teams and Florida key religious leaders. This conference helped identify and address any hindrances to cooperation, especially during times of foreign disaster relief.

Though different religious groups were invited, the participants were Christian. Pastor Rick Warren wrote an article of the power of the church, "The Church—the greatest force on Earth."

He notes that the Church has eight distinct advantages over the efforts of business and government:

1. The Church provides for the largest participation More than 2 billion people claim to be followers of Jesus Christ.
2. The Church provides for the widest distribution. The church is more widely spread—more widely distributed-than any business franchise in the world.
3. The Church provides the longest continuation.

The Church has been around for 2,000 years. The church is not a fly-by-night operation. The Church has a track record that spans centuries: Malicious leaders have tried to destroy it, hostile groups have persecuted it, and skeptics have scoffed at it. Nevertheless, God's Church is bigger now than ever before in history.

Why? Because it's the Church that Jesus established, and it is indestructible. The Bible calls the Church an unshakable kingdom. In Matthew 16:18, Jesus says, "I will build my Church and all the powers of hell will not conquer it" (NLT). All the powers of hell—in other words, no hurricane, no earthquake, no tsunami, no famine, no pandemic, no army will ever conquer the Church established by Jesus Christ.

4.   The Church provides the fastest expansion

Even in countries that are closed to traditional Christian missions, the church continues to expand. Tackling issues like poverty, disease, or illiteracy must be addressed by something growing faster than the problem.

5.   The Church provides the highest motivation

The church is motivated by love. Jesus stated it as the Great Commandment: Love God with all your heart and love your neighbor as yourself. It is love that never gives up; it is love that keeps moving forward despite the appearance of impossible odds; and it is love that outlasts any problem.

6.   The Church provides the strongest authorization

God authorized the Church to take on global giants, such as spiritual lostness, egocentric leadership, poverty, disease, and ignorance. With God's authorization, the outcome is guaranteed to be successful.

7.   The Church provides the simplest administration

The Church is organized in such a way that we can network faster and with less bureaucracy than most governmental agencies or even well-meaning charities.

8.   The Church provides for God's conclusion

Jesus said in Matthew 24:14, "The good news about God's Kingdom will be preached in all the world to every nation, and then the end will come." It is inevitable and unavoidable.[13]

This perspective is important. Each religious group—those in the country affected and concerned believers in the United States have a tremendous ministry impact, something that neither government nor business can compare.

This conference was held in the new SOUTHCOM facility built in 2010. The previous building, the one I first entered in 2008 was a rented facility. In December 2010, the new $402 million headquarters was opened. Sitting a few hundred yards away from the old building, the new building encompasses more than 39 football fields of office space. The main building has four stories that contain numerous offices, 20 conference rooms and eight training rooms.

We held our conference at the adjoining 45,000-square-foot "Conference Center of the Americas," which can support meetings of differing classification levels and multiple translations, information sources and video conferencing. As noted in the Miami media, "This will support engagement and cooperative activities with military and security forces from across the Americas, ranging from multinational humanitarian assistance operations and military exercises to bilateral training and subject-matter-expert exchanges."[14]

I was honored to be a participant and leader in the "Partnership of the Americas" as we engaged with religious leaders, nationally and internationally, in order to bring a remarkable "unity of effort."

PERSONAL TRANSITIONS

A transition was looming. As mentioned, Congress has established what is called a "1095 rule" for Reservists on ManDay (MPA) orders in order to be on full-time status. Reservists like myself could only serve 1,095 days in a rolling four-year calendar. Waivers were extremely rare. (The Fiscal Year 2022 National Defense Authorization Act extended this to 1,825 days.)

While at SOUTHCOM, I had the opportunity to address the US Air Force Academy (USAFA) Parents' Club. This organization provides opportunities for parents and families to support USAFA Cadet candidates, appointees, and Prep School candidates. I was asked to provide an inspirational speech for the students in the audience who were preparing for their Air Force adventure. The words below provide a challenge to those gathered and reflect upon my Air Force adventure—at least to this point—as well.

AFA PARENT'S CLUB

Deer Creek Country Club, South Florida

"Thank you for the opportunity to come tonight and share with you in this occasion. We gather together as students, parents, friends as links in a long chain of military heritage. It is an honor to be a part of the U.S. Military, a military that has existed for over 220 years.

Just yesterday, our country reflected on the 65th anniversary of the historic D-Day landing on the shores of Normandy on June 6, 1944.

On that night, paratroopers were packed into C-47s, deep over occupied France. The band of brothers with the 101st Airborne anxiously awaited the call to jump. Many carried a letter from Gen. Eisenhower that they keep tucked under helmets, in jump boots, and in bulging jacket pockets.

It read: "Soldiers, Sailors, and Airmen of the Allied Expeditionary Force! You are about to embark upon the Great Crusade, toward which we have striven these many months. The eyes of the world are upon you."[15]

On this night of nights, these brave men were about to take a leap of historic proportions.

You can only imagine what was going through the minds of these young men. They were about to jump into the dark abyss with a well-armed enemy waiting below. They faced an uncertain future when they landed, but they were ready to complete the mission that they had trained and prepared to do.

Tonight, in this gathering at the Deer Creek Country Club, eyes are upon you as well. Like these of the 101st Airborne, you have also striven for many months, even years to come to take this leap. Eyes are upon you with prayers, support, and admiration for what is in store for you in your great adventure.

As you take this leap, what does it mean? What does it mean to serve? Four things that you should know.

Know that you are part of something bigger than yourself

When those men of the 101st Airborne were about to jump into the uncertain abyss, they were not jumping out of selfish ambition, they were willing to take the leap and land on some hostile ground because of a cause bigger than themselves. They were repeating the acts of our forefathers who took up arms in the name of freedom since the Revolutionary War, the Great Wars and those that followed—Vietnam, Korea, the Persian Gulf, Iraq, Afghanistan.

You are a link in the rich history of those who are willing to take a stand for the cause of freedom. And, unlike some before you, you have volunteered to take the leap.

Some may think you are a little crazy for choosing this path—but it is a noble one, one reserved for the few. The dream is becoming a reality. Though you have the dream and motivation, training is needed as well. In the military, we don't just try, we train.

Most of my Air Force Career has been spent in training environments—training young men and women to enter and function in the Air Force. For ten years I was assigned to Lackland Air Force Base, called the Gateway to the Air Force because it is the entry point for all enlisted, I then was assigned to Randolph AFB to minister to pilots and navigators in training.

In 1998, I participated in a special tour at the U.S. Air Force Academy and ministered to the young cadets who were participating in the second phase of the Basic Cadet Training, or the BCT, or as it is affectionately called, "The Beast" in the field environment of Jack's Valley. There, senior Academy students were under the watch-care of instructors to shoulder the responsibility for training of incoming freshmen.

What is true at Lackland is especially true at the Academy—young men and women are brought to the limits of their endurance, physically, mentally, emotionally, spiritually, and they come out the better for it. The drills, the marching, the customs are all designed to remind the cadet that they are more than just individuals, they are a team, united in one purpose.

The way you see the world will change. Instead of seeing life through a very limited sight vision, it will expand.

Your life will be broader and deeper. One word of caution. When you come back and encounter people back home that have not received some of the training and perspective you have—don't be too hard on them.

You are part of something bigger than yourself.

Know that you will experience an uncommon camaraderie.

The Army calls it the battle buddy, the Navy calls it the shipmate, the Air Force calls it the Wingman. We take care of each other. At the Academy and throughout your Air Force career, you develop life-long friends. You will find yourself like your father or grandfather who has those cheesy, "Do you remember when…" stories. Those things that you once rolled your eyes about will be important to you.

Those activities become memories. These are memories you can share today and to the next generation.

Five years ago, the top generals in the United States Air Force had assembled at the Air Force Association's Air and Space Conference and Technology Exposition. A recurring theme at the conference was the size and shape of the Air Force of tomorrow. Though types of aircraft and technological advances garnished the most attention, General Jumper , the Chief of Staff of the United States Air Force was more focused on the individual Airman. He referred to an alarming suicide rate in the Air Force and he said, "Leaders can only do so much," he said. "It's the people who are best friends, who are intimate, who know when the problem reaches a critical stage. What we have to do is make sure our processes, procedures and programs increase our awareness of one another so intervention can happen at the right time." He later said, "It's the ethos of the wingman, where we have to depend on each other… and our first charge is to take care of one another."[12]

In this "sight vision" from the top general, two observations are worth noting. First, humans are more important than machines. To the uninformed, it may appear the military is more concerned about bombs and bullets than it is about individual Airmen. Though technology will continue to explode with new innovations, the heart of America's military is its people. The General used the term "Airman" which in Air Force terminology encompasses all ranks, all jobs, and all positions. All are important—from the Airman Basic fresh out of Basic Training to the top generals—the success of the United States Air Force rests on each of them.

The second observation from the General's speech is that Airmen in the United States Air Force look out for each other—it is the "ethos of the wingman". It is the way things are done.

The ancient Romans were the first to document the importance of the wingman.

The most basic Roman battle lines were arranged with the infantry in the center and cavalry on the wings. The main purpose of the cavalry was to protect the center from being outflanked. For the Army to succeed, it was imperative that the infantry and cavalry understood and followed a prearranged plan and moved with a single purpose. Separately, neither the infantry nor the cavalry stood much chance at defeating an opponent, but together, watching out for each other, they were a formidable force.

Beyond the Roman Army would be the original wingmen, birds themselves.

Geese and some other species of birds migrate in distinctive "V" or "U" formations or in lines. By taking advantage of the wing tip vortex of the bird in front, each bird can save energy by reducing drag. The energy savings in flight can be as much as 50%. Researchers have discovered that a flock of 25 birds in formation can fly 70 percent farther than a single bird using the same amount of energy.

Pilots know the migrating birds' mechanism as the "wing tip vortex." The volume of air surrounding a bird must always remain the same, so when a bird displaces air downward on a wing beat, some air also must be displaced upward.

This upward displacement of air creates an upwash beyond a bird's wing tips that enables the bird beside or behind it to fly with a bit less energy, like a hang-glider who catches an updraft of warm air. To increase efficiency, they also rotate positions to allow all of the flock to benefit.[16]

In a world that says, "Its all about me, my needs are the most important..." the military reminds us that though each individual is important, we respect and need the person by our side—our battle buddy, our shipmate, our wingman.

You are part of something bigger than yourself.

You will experience an uncommon camaraderie.

Know that leadership will be developed

There is a debate whether leaders are born or made. I believe it is both. There are some people, when they walk into a room, people are immediately drawn to them. For others, it is a process of learning and confidence.

Leadership is key in the Air Force—from the Basic Training Airman to the top General. From the pilots who fly to the technicians who maintain their aircraft. Leadership is key.

You will be given jobs in your early twenties that would be unheard of from your high school friends. These responsibilities will demand leadership.

At the core of your leadership will be your character.

Air Force core values are based on ethics, a system of moral principles or values, which are hardly new. As far back in history as the 6th century BC, Greek philosophers including Pythagoras, Socrates, Plato and Aristotle, recognized the importance of goodness, duty, virtue, and obligation in the fullest harmonious development of human potential.

In modern times, the renowned military strategist

Carl Von Clausewitz identified two indispensable traits as essential to military genius "…first, an intellect that, even in the darkest hour, retains some glimmerings of the inner light which leads to truth; and second, the courage to follow this faint light wherever it may lead."[17]

> You are part of something bigger than yourself.
> You will experience an uncommon camaraderie.
> Leadership will be developed

Know that challenges and opportunities will come—seize the day!

Not going to lie and tell you that from now on everything will be smooth sailing—there will be challenging days in front of you. There will be days that you are not sure if you are going to make it. There will be days of disappointment—these are all a part of life—whether in or out of the military.

Keep the vision before you, keep striving forward.

In my Air Force adventure, I have been exposed to some great leaders and great adventures.

I have been in the heart of Cheyenne Mountain of NORAD.

I have been able to be a part of the celebration of life for Gordon Cooper—one of the original Mercury 7 Astronauts.

I have flown over the sands of Nevada in a KC-135.

While at SOUTHCOM, I have been able to serve in Panama, Guantanamo Bay, Belize, Honduras and other places in our Area of Responsibility.

You will have your own stories, own experiences—look forward to them, seize them!

I close with words from the famous poem "High Flight" by Pilot Officer John Gillespie Magee, Jr. Gillespie was an American serving with the Royal Canadian Air Force during WWII. The son of missionary parents, he earned a scholarship to Yale but enlisted in the RCAF to become a pilot.

He wrote these words on the back of an envelope after his first solo in a Spitfire:

Oh! I have slipped the surly bonds of earth
And danced the skies on laughter-silvered wings;
Sunward I've climbed, and joined the tumbling mirth
Of sun-split clouds—and done a hundred things
You have not dreamed of—
wheeled and soared and swung
High in the sunlit silence. Hov'ring there,
I've chased the shouting wind along, and flung
My eager craft through footless halls of air.
Up, up the long, delirious, burning blue
I've topped the wind-swept heights with easy grace
Where never lark, or even eagle flew -
And, while with silent lifting mind I've trod
The high untrespassed sanctity of space,
Put out my hand and touched the face of God.[18]

Congratulations on taking the leap and experiencing the great adventure.

Many more days will come. Keep pressing on. In the words of Joshua of old, "Be strong and courageous, for the Lord your God will be with you wherever you go."

STEPS OF TRANSITION

My 1095 days were complete. I was now fully trained, I was familiar with the systems, I knew the people, I embraced the mission, and yet I had to leave. Waivers to extend were not an option. In my corner of the world, it didn't make sense. God and the military had another plan. My transition plan, and let me emphasize, my plan, was to get back to Texas and step into a denominational ministry position or a pastoral position in a local church. Another option was to take a deployment, something I had always wanted to do, but never seemed to have the opportunity. A deployment opportunity had arisen at the forward operating base of US Central Command. It was also a Deputy Command Chaplain position doing work similar to what I had performed at SOUTHCOM.

Though Susie had considered staying in South Florida during the 6-month deployment, we both decided it made sense to move back to Texas, to the north-Dallas suburb of Richardson, where she was close to her sister, brother-in-law, and mom. So, movers packed us up, and we moved to an apartment in Richardson. While I was awaiting my deployment, there were still several steps needing to be taken. One step was to empty out a storage unit in Dickinson. Because of a lack of space, we stored items in this unit for three years. Our son, Blake came down from Denver. He and some other First Baptist Church, Dickinson church members helped pack the U-Haul.

Once packed, Blake and I were on our way to the Dallas metroplex. As I drove, I looked over to my son who was sitting in the seat next to me. For those who have read my previous book in this trilogy, "The Marshall Chronicles: Farm to Market Edition," you may recall the book beginning with me driving a U-Haul to my first pastorate with 10-month-old Blake sitting in the seat next to me. (Again, to reiterate, I know now that a 10-month-old should not be traveling in a U-Haul, but it was the '80s and we were somewhat ignorant about those things!) Anyway, instead of 10-month-old Blake, now sat 25 year old, Blake. I could not help but think about all that had taken place in our family and in my pastoral/chaplain career. Where did the time go?

Christmas 2011 was probably the most stressful because the time of deployment was drawing near. In fact, the next morning, December 26th, after Blake dropped me off at Love Field Airport in Dallas, I flew to Baltimore. The next morning, I joined a group of military members who flew on a commercial flight from Baltimore, had a brief stop at Aviano, Italy, and then on to Al Udeid Air Base in Doha, Qatar.

Al Udeid Air Base

2011

In the Desert

ARRIVAL AT O'DARK THIRTY

The Al Udeid Air Base is a military base located west of Doha Qatar and is owned by the Qatar Emiri Air Force. It is home to the forward headquarters of United States Air Forces Central Command, the Combined Air and Space Operations Center, and the 379th Air Expeditionary Wing.[1] 8000—10,000 personnel are stationed there.

Built on a flat stretch of desert about 20 miles southwest of the Qatari capital Doha, Al-Udeid Air Base once was considered so sensitive that American military officers identified it as only being somewhere in southwest Asia. Even during my deployment, we would were instructed identify it as an "undisclosed location." I thought that was curious because the small Base Exchange on base sold coffee cups and t-shirts proudly displaying the words, "Al Udeid Air Base."

Over the years, the secrecy and sensitivity have diminished. Today, the sprawling hub is designed to showcase the Gulf Arab emirate's tight security partnership with the United States. The Qataris have continued to pour money into the base — more than $8 billion since 2003.[1]

At Al Udeid, there were two separate Chaplain Corps teams. The first team was at the base level. Al Udeid was the largest base under the Central Command (CENTCOM.) It employed several chaplains and chaplain assistants in meeting the spiritual needs of the base. They held Worship Services, conducted unit engagements, provided counseling, and served under the Wing Commander.

The second team was assigned to the Combined Air and Space Operations Center (CAOC) under leadership of the Central Command. This chaplain team provided religious advisement to the Air Force Central Command (AFCENT) Commander and provided Command oversight to each of the bases spread throughout the Middle East and the CENTCOM AOR. I was part of this team. The team included the Command Chaplain, Ch, Col Dondi Costin, two chaplain assistants and myself. I was the lone reservist on the team, the other three were Active Duty. I had actually served with Ch Costin at Lackland years prior. He was impressive as a Captain and had risen through the ranks. Ch Costin and CMSGT Peters had a robust travel schedule. MSgt Laufer and I primarily handled issues and questions from the field. I represented Ch Costin at briefings and other meetings when he traveled, engaging with Chaplain Corps personnel throughout the region.

Like my time at SOUTHCOM, for a reservist, this was a tremendous opportunity, and I felt honored to be selected to serve in this strategic position.

In an attempt to maintain communication back home and share some deployment detail to my family, friends, and former church members, I sent a series of emails describing my experiences. I will use these emails as a background in sharing some of my days at Al Udeid.

DEPLOYMENT EMAILS

Email 1—January 8, 2012

Hey gang,

I wanted to let you know that my feet are firmly on the ground for my military "Great Adventure." I thought that, now and then, I would drop you a note and maybe a picture or two. I took a broad swath of my email/facebook contacts that entails the "to" line above. Feel free to forward this email to anyone else you think might be interested—also let me know so that I can add them to my list.

As family and friends, you are all appreciated. All of you have had some impact on my life. I appreciate your love, friendship, and prayers. During the next few months, I would like to share some of the experiences/impressions that I have. Because of the nature of the work, the details will probably be somewhat broad. For the pastors/staff members out there, I would appreciate the prayers of your church, not only for me but for all of our military members during these uncertain times.

Susie is in Richardson, Tx. If you are in the area, I know she would appreciate a visit...and lift some prayers up to her while I am away.
Take care,
Randy

Email 2—January 11, 2012

Hey gang,

Thanks for allowing me to share some thoughts. Let me start with the basics—where I live and what I eat! There are three types of accommodations here—tents, trailers, and dorms. I currently live in a trailer (long trailer with several individual rooms). The room is not bad, just small—about the size of a prison cell! However, it has a bed and heating/air conditioner, so for a deployment, that's pretty good! Eventually, I will move to a nicer dorm. (I thought about taking a picture of the tents and tell you that I was living in them just to make you feel sorry for me, but, you know...integrity). I do walk to the bathroom and shower—that's roughing it! Meals are served in the Dining Facility (DFAC) (Everything in the military has an abbreviation). Because I am on orders, there is no cost for the food. The meals are decent and they are all you can eat! Looking around the base, there are rocks everywhere—not much sand. I thought I would practice my golf sand shots—but not to be. Another oddity here is the time difference. I am 9 hours ahead of Central time. I call Susie around 8:00 or 9:00p.m. my time and talk to her about 11:00am or 12 noon. I tell her to have a great day and she tells me "good night!" All for now!
Thanks for all of you!
Randy

The housing accommodations did get better. A few weeks into the deployment, I was able to move to the dorms. The contrast between the two was significant. The trailers were individual units that contained a bunk bed and little else. Taking a shower or using the restroom required a walk to the restroom/shower facility, affectionately known as "the Cadillac." Though there was a bunk, based on my rank, I was able to have a private room—not everyone was that fortunate. The dorms on the other hand were modern two-story facilities. Rooms were more comfortable. There was an indoor area to gather. Each room had a shared kitchenette and shared restroom/shower with the individual in the adjoining room.

As mentioned, I was assigned to the CAOC. The CAOC is the command and control center of the CENTCOM AOR that brings airpower to the fight. The set-up was similar to my PANAMAX experience at SOUTHCOM. In an oversized room, tables were set up with computers and government phones. At the computers were personnel representing various functions—logistics, plans, personnel, medical, legal, chaplain, etc…The room was arranged so that some were lined up in the middle, and others, like our area was on the perimeter. From my desk, I had a clear view of the entire room. Men and women were at work making sure needed information, supplies, and guidance was given to those downrange in various locations. The biggest difference between my experience in the PANAMAX exercise and this experience was that this was no computer simulation. There were men and women downrange who were experiencing incredible stress and facing imminent danger. This was the real deal. There was a sober reminder that what I was doing impacted lives.

I spent part of my days communicating and coordinating with the chaplains with the Air Force Personnel Center (AFPC) in San Antonio, TX. It was their job to fill all Chaplain Corps personnel slots. These slots were filled by Active Duty, Air National Guard, and Reserve Components—a true Total Force endeavor! Once the six-month deployment was complete, orders would be "cut" and the deployers would go home, or in military lingo, "redeploy." They would be replaced by another set of personnel. My job was at least threefold: First, keep track of Chaplain Corps members who were coming and going. This required communication with AFPC. Second, serve in Ch Costin's place when he traveled. This mainly consisted of staff meetings and senior leader engagement. Third, maintain communication with Air Force personnel down range and field any questions they may have

In my communication with Chaplain teams, most dealt with questions concerning administrative items. Some communicated prayer requests. Sometimes, I assisted in dealing with religious accommodation issues. Religion in the military is extremely diverse. In the Air Force alone, there are over 160 different religions and denominations identified. One of the key responsibilities of the Chaplain Corps is to guarantee member's religious expression based on First Amendment rights. Commanders are bound to honor these rights unless there is a duty requirement. Chaplains are key advisors to the commander concerning religious accommodation issues.

When dealing with religious accommodation issues, well-established policies and procedures are followed. Occasionally, the issue is outside of the norm and some clarifications are needed. In my position, as a senior leader, I could be a resource. Perhaps the most interesting out-of-the-box question came from a chaplain who was trying to negotiate the needs of a Pastafarian. Pastafarianism is not recognized by the Department of Defense as a true religion. Adherents tend to see it as a satire, a light-hearted view of religion. Interestingly enough, Pastafarianism, also called the "Church of the

Flying Spaghetti Monster", has international branches. Pastafarians have used their claimed faith as a test case to argue for freedom of religion, and to oppose government discrimination against people who do not follow a recognized religion.

Apparently, at a local base, one of the members had approached the chaplain and claimed he sincerely held to this belief and desired accommodation to practice. The chaplain sent an email to myself and Ch Costin, requesting assistance. Though I was 99 percent sure the member was just messing with the chaplain, I considered the request and sent the following email.

> Ch _____,
> Thanks for the information. Ch Costin is out of the country. We certainly live in a time of multiplicity of ideas and concepts. Not knowing the level of sincerity of the requester, and avoiding the debate of the definition of religion (at least at this point), let me share a couple of thoughts that would apply to religious accommodation of all faith groups:
>
> 1. Our role as chaplains is to "provide" or "provide for" the religious needs of authorized personnel. Faith expressions outside of our tradition require us to accommodate, but do not require us to participate.
> 2. Rely on DoD Directive 1300.17. As you know, it prescribes policy, procedures and responsibilities for the accommodation of religious practices in the military services.
>
> - Para 3.1 states: "It is DoD policy that requests for accommodation of religious practices should be approved by commanders when accommodation will not have an adverse impact on military readiness, unit cohesion,

standards, or discipline"

- It is the Air Force's policy to approve requests for accommodation of religious practices when the request does not have an adverse impact on readiness, unit cohesion, health, safety, discipline or otherwise interfere with the airman's military duties (AFI 52-101)

Suggested action steps:

1. Personally contact (member) and ask him what he is desiring. I suggest you bring (chaplain assistant) with you.
2. Remind him that faith expressions in the military are very diverse. It is impossible to have "religious activities" tailor-made for each group; however, inform him that he is free to practice his faith assuming that it complies with the directive above.
3. Perusing the (Pastafarian) website, it appears that Fridays are religious holidays. If personnel are given a day off and the mission is not impacted, he can request Friday as his day off.
4. Also in perusing the website, it is clear that Pastafarians interact and encourage participation from other faith groups. Invite him to one of your worship services. At the very least, it could open of door of interesting conversation.

Hope this helps! Let me know how it plays out,
Ch Marshall

This email is an example of handling things at the lowest level. Talk to the member and give some options. If the member is still not satisfied, it could be elevated to the next level. I didn't hear anything else, so I believe it was settled. Good thing. I would hate to be the chaplain that has to explain the need to accommodate someone wanting to worship a Flying Spaghetti Monster!

Email 3—January 21, 2012

Greetings again from Southwest Asia!

I wanted to share a couple of things about military chaplaincy in general. Chaplains have been around since the Revolutionary War. The intent is to provide a sort of moral compass to military members and to guarantee their first amendment right of freedom of worship. Chaplains provide not only military support (preaching, teaching, counseling, visitation, etc..) but also military advisement to commanders. Every chaplain is endorsed by a religious body/denomination. So, a chaplain like myself endorsed by the Baptist General Convention of Texas represents that body to the military. I am not asked (or ordered) to do anything that violates my conscience of tradition. Saying that, I also provide ministry to a vast array of theological backgrounds. Of course, there are those who are unchurched and/or have no faith background. A large percentage, around 30% claim "no preference" to religious beliefs.

The military is a microcosm of our society. Many are searching, and especially among the young Airmen that I speak, they are open to spiritual conversations. Please pray for these informal conversations that I have, not only with the younger Airmen but high-ranking officers that I regularly interact. In the position that I have here, I also have the opportunity to have regular conversations with our chaplains who are deployed throughout the region. Some are in some very remote and dangerous locations. I would appreciate your prayers for me as I mentor and encourage them, as well as prayers for these chaplains and chaplain assistants.

I am attaching a video of some Americans and British military members enjoying their Christmas together in Afghanistan. God is working in our midst, pray for the Spirit of the Lord to envelope all of the Persian Gulf and Southwest Asia for His glory!
Thanks for letting me share,
Randy

Email 4—Feb 1, 2012

All,

Hope you are having a great Sunday. The personnel located here not only include other Services (Army, Navy, and Marines) but also Coalition members. I was sitting next to a French officer at an official function last night and struck up a conversation. I asked him what city he was from (as if I would know any city in France besides Paris—he actually said, "Paris".) I told him that I was from Texas. He looked at me and said, "I'm a bit confused." I leaned in a little closer. He said, "Are you from the United States or are you from Texas?"

It took me a second before I realized that he was making a joke! He said that he knew that Texas was once its own country. I said, "Well you certainly know your Texas history."

He replied in his thick French accent, "Oh yes, I have learned a lot about Texas from watching John Wayne and J.R. Ewing." Certainly, two of our greatest Texas ambassadors!

If you are looking for a way to send some support to our troops, I'll pass along one idea. There is a coffee house called "Green Beans Coffee" at many deployed locations. They have a program called "Cup of Joe for a Joe" where you can donate $2.00 and buy a cup of coffee for an anonymous Soldier, Sailor, Airman, or Marine. The deployed member receives a notification from the company with a code that they take to the coffee shop. You can also write a note of encouragement and appreciation. So, if you have $2.00 to spare, its one way to show your appreciation. The website is www.greenbeanscoffee.com. I realize that it is somewhat of a marketing tool and we all wish we had thought of it, but nevertheless the cup of coffee and note of encouragement is appreciated by the Joe (or Jane) in deployed settings.

All for now! Take care!

Randy

BACK AT THE CAOC...

The work I did was serious, but there was some levity as well. As mentioned, some of the days were slower than others. In this large, multi-disciplinary room, there were plenty of opportunities for social interaction. Relationships with Public Affairs (PA), Attorneys (JA) and Chaplains (Ch) and Medical (SG) were commonplace—mainly because each discipline served as a commander's resource with Religious Accommodation issues. These were part of the commander's "special staff." More on that later. Each of these "special staff" directorates were on the perimeter of the CAOC and each area had a mounted flatscreen television set. These televisions were designed to inform on news with an occasional check of some area of interest. I discovered that my television remote not only controlled my T.V., but also the T.V. across the room at the Public Affairs area. Since we had a good relationship with Public Affairs, and just to be mischievous, one day, I looked over the top of my computer screen and pointed the remote at their T.V., changing the channel. Someone noticed the change and changed it back. After a few minutes, I changed it again.

They changed it back. I changed it again. Finally, with my remote in hand, and with a smile, I went to them and confessed. They probably did not expect the chaplain to be so devious! Personally, I would consider this a "creative observation." After hearing the chaplain's "confession," I was forgiven.

Email 5—February 12, 2012

All,

Hope you are having a great Sunday! Weather here has been in the '60s but is slowing warming—should be nice and toasty by the time I leave. A lot of chaplain ministry depends on building relationships and trust—really, a deployment is a perfect environment for this. The base chapel here is showing the movie "Courageous" on February 14th. Pray for renewed relationships both for families and a fresh encounter with God.

I am attaching a conversation that I had with a young pilot a couple of weeks ago and a devotional thought—Hopefully, these words can encourage you as you daily represent our Lord!

All for now! Take care!

Randy

Below is the account with the young pilot and a short devotion:

A DFAC DISCOVERY

You never know what you will discover in the DFAC (Dining Facility.) The DFAC (pronounced "DeeFac") is a building where meals—breakfast, lunch, and supper—are served.

Like a lot of cafeteria settings, the food is not always great, but there's a lot of it! So, usually, three times a day I make my way to the DFAC. I walk in to pick out a tray which will hold my fork, knife, spoon and plate—yes, this is fine dining. Depending on what looks good, I will then stand and wait in the hot food line, deli line, salad bar line, etc… For most meals, I go to the DFAC with a group of people. Some meals—particularly breakfast, I go by myself.

One morning, for breakfast I got my plate of eggs and cup of coffee, sat next to a young officer and initiated a conversation. I asked him where he was from. He told me his base of assignment. He also told me that he was a pilot, a graduate of Baylor University (located in Waco, TX) on a six-month deployment. Remember, a deployment draws men and women from all over the United States, and with Coalition Forces, from all over the world. So, to randomly sit next to a young man who graduated from Baylor was remarkable in itself. I then asked where he grew up—he replied, "Central Texas." Again, being the prodding chaplain, I asked, "where in Central Texas?" He said that I probably never heard of it, a little town called Evant (Long e with the accent on the e). I looked at him and said, "I know exactly where Evant is." I went on to tell him that I attended Howard Payne University in Brownwood. During my senior year I had a student pastorate at the Fairview Baptist Church in Evant. I would get up early (for a college student), drive 60 miles past the towns of Zepher, Mullin, Goldthwaite, and Star to preach to ten members who faithfully attended each Sunday morning (eleven when Susie, my girlfriend, later my wife came along.) I was paid $50.00 a week to preach a sermon that was probably worth 50 cents.

After church we would all go to the church patriarch's house and eat chicken fried steak, mashed potatoes, and homemade pie!

Some things you just don't forget—I know where Evant, Texas is! This young pilot looked at me incredulously. Evant has a population of 393 people on a good day. Fairview Baptist Church is located just west of Evant on County Rd 527. Here were two men, sitting in a deployed location, across the ocean in the middle of the Persian Gulf who happened to strike up a conversation in the DFAC—fellow believers, fellow Baptists, and fellow Texans with a connection to a small town of a population less than 400 located over 8000 miles away! You never know what you will discover in the DFAC. He smiled and said that he would definitely tell this story next year at his 10-year high school reunion.

Perhaps you have heard of "six degrees of separation". It is the idea that everyone on earth is approximately six steps away from any other person on earth, so that a chain of "a friend of a friend" statements can be made to connect any two people in six steps or fewer. My brain is not big enough to grasp this; however, I can think of several examples of conversations where I walk away in amazement thinking, "What are the odds of that?" This breakfast conversation reminded me of the account of Elijah's culinary encounter recorded in I Kings 19:1-18. It is a remarkable story of the fearful, despondent Elijah and his rejuvenation from a meal served in a remote, personal, God-delivered DFAC. His renewal of physical strength by a simple meal eaten under a juniper tree in the wilderness led to an even more remarkable spiritual renewal in a cave located in Horeb, the mountain of God. In the midst of the prophet's despair, God reminded Elijah that he was not alone— Elijah was protected under the care of God, and supported by seven thousand other believers who were ready to stand with him. For all of us, life can take its toll. Like the prophet Elijah, who was on his own self-imposed deployment, we can also find ourselves emotionally tired, physically exhausted, and spiritually spent.

Apply his lesson learned—"stop trying to do it all alone." In the midst of the turmoil of life's responsibilities, when the load seems to be overwhelming, be aware of the presence of the Almighty. Listen to His voice, which is oftentimes a quiet whisper spoken as you interpret life's events through the filter of God's Word. Being sensitive to the Spirit of God, you may sense Him relaying something real "spiritual" like, "You need to take a nap and when you get up, drink some water and eat a sandwich!" If you listen very closely, you may also hear the question that rang in Elijah's ears, "What are you doing here?" God is asking the prophet, why are you afraid? Why are you running? Don't you know that I am here with you, and to top it off, there are seven thousand other believers who are ready to stand with you?

Believer, take a breath and lean on the presence of God. Drink from His Living Water, eat from His Banquet table, be refreshed in His presence once again. Each of us has God-appointed tasks to fulfill his Commission in our corner of the world. We are designed to minister in His power with a realization that "we are surrounded by a cloud of witnesses" who are cheering us on and a vast army of believers, from one to six degrees of separation, who are by our side. It's a new day, Listen to the voice of God wherever you find yourself today… even in the DFAC, you never know what you will discover…

BACK AT THE CAOC...

I was speaking with a female Airman who worked in Public Affairs. She mentioned she had spent a month in Haiti during Operation UNIFIED RESPONSE. I told her of some of my experiences during that time when I was at SOUTHCOM. The subject turned to faith. She said that she didn't really hold to any belief. I replied that I would like to talk with her more about that. She said, "that would be fine as long as I was open to discussion and didn't think I had all the answers." I told her that I hold to some basic truths. I continued to say that a person couldn't have a true faith without strong beliefs. I emphasized that people should be able to have an open, civil dialogue when discussing beliefs. We were able to converse periodically throughout the tour. Hopefully, the conversations were beneficial and her understanding of faith was changed, at least to see that a civil conversation about faith was possible.

Far from a faith conversation, I also spoke with another young Airman. In the conversation, he said he was from New York. I replied, "I guess you are a Giants fan." He said, "actually, I am a Jets fan." So, I asked him, "what is the difference between a Giants fan and a Jets fan?" He said, "Chaplain, it's like this…if you want to make a business deal, you take someone to a Giants game. If you want to get drunk, you take him to a Jets game."

Yes, two divergent conversations! As a chaplain, I have always been amazed at what people will say! I did consider it a refreshing that each conversation was open and honest, and they were willing to express their thoughts to their chaplain.

Email 6—February 25, 2012

Whew!

As you can see from the news, a lot is going on in our region.

Tensions continue to rise over Iran's nuclear program.

Syrian protests, government crackdowns and world outrage continues to escalate.

Angry protests are building and boiling over in Afghanistan.

I know in the states, these stories (and various subplots) continue to be front page headlines and commentary fodder.

When you read these news accounts and every time you fill up your gas tank with even more expensive gas…I want to encourage you to say a prayer.

Pray for our world and national leaders.

Pray for people in the world that are facing needless suffering.

Pray for our missionaries who serve in the crossfire.

Pray for our strategic-level military officers.

Pray for all of our military members, especially those in harm's way.

Pray for our chaplains and chaplain assistants as they seek to calm fears and speak a word of truth in the midst of some uncertain and volatile times.

Diplomacy and military might have their place. However, I firmly believe that the prayer of a righteous man and woman is much more powerful and effective (James 5:16). Let's appropriate our privilege to come before the Father!

I am attaching a picture of a hand-sized case that holds my ID, cell phone, keys, etc…On the front, inside the plastic is a "Shield of Strength" dog tag that says, "Though my enemies attack me, I will not fear, though battles rage around me, I will still trust in God," which is a rough translation of Psalm 27:3. The other day, someone spontaneously asked me for a thought of the day, I replied with one of my favorite verses, "Be strong and courageous, do not tremble, do not be dismayed for the Lord your God will be with you wherever you go." Joshua 1:9. "Be strong and courageous" is repeated three times in Joshua 1 and various times throughout Scripture. True strength and courage can only be found in our everlasting God!

I know that some of you are going through some personal battles today. Keep your eyes on Him, do not fear, be strong, be courageous!

Till next time,

Randy

BACK IN THE CAOC...

In this email, I mentioned angry protests boiling over in Afghanistan. What I did not mention is one of our Central Command Bases was at the heart of the issue—Bagram Airfield near the capital city of Kabul. In February, two Afghan American interpreters at the base removed 1652 damaged books and Islamic texts from the library at the Parwan Detention Facility and boxed them for storage. On 22 September, U.S. troops sent them to the incinerator to be burned, a culturally insensitive and potentially explosive decision. Several Afghan garbage collectors working at the base reported finding a number of charred books and notified an Afghan National Army commander. The word spread. Outraged Afghans besieged the base, raining it with Molotov cocktails and stones. After five days of protest, 30 people had been killed, including four Americans. Over 200 people were wounded. Riots continued throughout the region.

A small group of troops caused an international situation. A saying came out of this event: "Tactical decisions have strategic results." An action at the local level can cause a (in this case, literal) firestorm. We assisted Chaplain Corps members by checking on their well-being and giving guidance on how to handle the situation.

On a lighter side...

Daily, as I scanned the sea of Air Force uniforms, heads were down, quietly typing reports and answering emails from downrange; requesting and requesting information, communicating issues that needed to be addressed, etc...

One day, the power in the CAOC went out. The emergency generators kicked on, so the lights were on. But the computers were off. Something amazing happened. People actually started talking with each other. Some of the communication was business related, some discussed the inconvenience of not having computer access, some began to talk about memories of other experiences like this. Bewildered looks became smiling faces as they took an unexpected break. The problem was solved in less than thirty minutes and heads were back down tending to the task at hand. Something to think about. We all need to take a look around now and then, and maybe even talk to a human sometimes!

Email 7—March 18, 2012

It's "March Madness" baby!
Yes, even though we are 8000 miles away, March Madness is in full force on bases across Southwest Asia. Thanks to my Brother-in-Law, Bob's tournament bracket

on the web, I am connected to family, friends, and friends of friends in a friendly competition. The chaplain that I work with here is a huge North Carolina fan—he went to high school with Michael Jordan. So, of course he chose North Carolina to win it all. I chose Kentucky, which didn't win me any points with him! Our location is nine hours ahead of Central Standard Time. Like all sporting events, many games are shown live here and then repeated during the day on the "Armed Forces Network (AFN)" In order to watch an evening game (broadcasted in the states) live, I would need to get up in the early morning.

There are many ways that Soldiers, Airmen, Marines, and Seamen keep connected—Skype, phone calls, letters, packages, email, facebook—some very traditional ways, some that would have been unimaginable just a few years ago. Staying connected is important, because while the Service member is performing his/her duty here, life back home continues. At chapel, I heard prayer requests like:

- Pray for my wife, she is due with our son next week.

- Pray for my mother-in-law, she was diagnosed with cancer.

- Pray that I can get through the next few weeks...

Privately, I have heard concerns about wayward children, unfaithful spouses, finances, physical health, spiritual health, and careers. Concerning careers, the military continues to downsize; however, requirements seem to be on the upside. Like many, the military continues to do more with less. But let me say, you can be proud of the sacrifice, work, expertise, and professionalism of our military men and women—they do some incredible things under incredible conditions.

I am also attaching a picture of me in my typical outdoor look here. Most of us wear these big sunglasses to either shield our eyes from the searing sun reflecting off

of the white rock/sand, or like today, to protect our eyes from being sand blasted from the 35-40 mph winds. At least the wind is keeping the flies away that showed up last week. It's around 85 degrees now, but I've been told it can reach around 125 degrees in the summer.
All for now, hope all is well there. Again, I appreciate each of you.
Randy

The days brought both days of boredom and days of intense operational tempo. In this environment, some questions arose concerning the struggle of a believer "loving your brother," and "defending your country." Feelings that may have been in the background of their minds are now front and center. Questions arise like, "How can I be an American warrior and a loving Christian?" or "How can I believe that every person is unique in the eyes of God, yet I am in a profession that ends lives?" These are honest and raw questions. I have been able to compare our military force to our local police force. We should always strive for peace; however, when trouble occurs and force is needed, we understand the need for a response. A tool that I have used since my days at Lackland is an explanation of the Just War Theory. These questions and struggles are not new to the church and to believers.

The Just-War Tradition provides an ethical and moral framework in understanding the rationale of military engagement. The United States upholds this tradition. Various Department of Defense Directives, codes of conduct, and rules of engagement are built upon the Just-War Tradition. This tradition is at least 2000 years old and is a result of contributions from philosophers, theologians, jurists, statesmen, and warriors. The Western tradition of Just War begins with the Roman statesman, Cicero who suggested some simple rules to determine if a war was just. Augustine of Hippo in the 4th century developed the Just-War idea even more. The Roman Emperor Constantine had legalized Christianity in AD 313 and encouraged its growth by his massive ecclesiastical building projects. Augustine, in contrast to many believers, felt that Christians had a responsibility to civic involvement. This included military involvement. He argued that Christian love at times demanded the use of force to restrain evil. For hundreds of years, the writings of Augustine provided Western civilization with its concept of the morality of war. The chief feature of this understanding was that at times a nation had a right, indeed a duty, to go to war. Having this framework of understanding with a rich theological tradition helped many military members as they navigated their Christian walk through a military culture. (See Flight Notes #6.)

As mentioned, I had daily phone conversations with Susie. The conversations were rarely long, just long enough to let her know all was fine. I would also learn any news about family and friends. I also discovered that my wife had become a Texas Rangers baseball fan. To my knowledge, before the deployment, she had never even watched a professional baseball game, much less had any interest. My deployment spawned an interest in watching baseball. She would watch any Texas Ranger game she could and was able to name the players in the regular batting rotation.

One day, during one of our regular calls, she seemed a bit distracted. I was telling her about some detail of my day, and I could hear her say, "Uh-huh, hmmm, Oh..." things like that. Finally, I asked her, "are you listening to me ?" She finally blurted out, "it's the bottom of the ninth, bases are loaded, and Hamilton is up to bat!" I appreciated her honesty. I mean, it's not like her husband is thousands of miles away in somewhat hostile territory, sacrificing for the freedoms of our country! I laughed and was glad that she had found a diversion while I was gone. At least her diversion was watching baseball on TV and not shopping at the mall!

ON THE FLIGHTLINE.

One of the difficult responsibilities of a minister is dealing with the sick and dying. Ministers are at key moments of people's lives. They are present when a baby is born. They provide baptisms. They celebrate communion. They perform weddings. Many times, they are present at anniversaries, birthdays, and other celebrations. Ministers are present in the good times as well as the bad.

As a local church pastor and chaplain, I performed more funerals than I can count. These are holy moments when the family and congregation are looking for hope and comfort. I have conducted military funerals at the base chapel. I have knocked on doors as part of the casualty notification team. During this deployment, I was also humbled to observe a dignified transfer of a Servicemember. A dignified transfer is what takes place at a base like Al Udeid. When a Servicemember is killed, a ramp ceremony takes place at the deployed location. The process is controlled by the Air Force Mortuary Affairs Operations office under the watchful eye of a senior officer. In order to give honor and respect, Airmen voluntarily gathered—many times in the early morning hours. They would fall into formation on the flight line. The mood is somber. As the aircraft lands, the formations tighten. Except for the aircraft's engine, there is silence.

On command, escorts begin to march toward the rear of the plane. The command, "present, arms" echoes among the ranks, and all salute. A vehicle arrives with the casket. On cue, the casket is lifted. The chaplain leads the procession to the rear of the aircraft. The chaplain provides a scripture and prayer before the casket is secured for the trip.

The chaplain and escorts then re-emerge and depart with the rest of the assembled Airmen.

This ceremony will be repeated at Dover AFB and between any stops that require a new aircraft.

The Airmen who are gathered may or may not know this Airman, but they are fully aware that war involves sacrifice and possibly, the ultimate sacrifice.

May we also be aware of the price of freedom.

Email 8—April 5, 2012

All,

Hope you are having a joyful "Holy Week." I have officially passed the half-way point in my deployment. Thanks again to all for your prayers. I feel like it has been productive and overall the time is moving quickly (for me, not for Susie!).

Just like in college, one of the highlights of the day is getting mail—especially packages! As chaplains we receive packages from individuals or organizations for us to distribute—a typical package has candy, cookies, magazines, etc... Sometimes we get personal "care packages" as well. This week, my sister, Sandy sent me a

"No place like Texas kit" that included Texas shaped crackers, girl scout cookies, a Frisbee and other things that remind me of home. She even sent me a toy 3x6 inch putting green—I put it on my desk because I love golf and it reminds me what grass looks like!

During this week preceding Easter Sunday, many Christian faith traditions honor Holy Thursday or Maundy Thursday. The strange word, "Maundy" is only used in reference to the observance of "Maundy Thursday" which commemorates the Last Supper and Jesus washing the feet of the apostles. The word "Maundy" means "mandate" or "commandment". It refers to Jesus' statement following the Lord's Supper—"A new commandment I give you, love one another. By this all men will know you are my disciples if you love one another." Hmm…maybe all of us should celebrate this mandate of love! We could undoubtedly advance the Kingdom further if we spent more time washing feet rather than twisting arms!

Take care,

Randy

I also included the following devotion that echoes the introduction of this book and describes the unique relationships among military chaplains.

A BAD JOKE GONE GOOD

A Priest, a Rabbi and a Minister walked into a room…

Though this may sound like the beginning of a bad joke, it is actually a snapshot in time from a current military deployment. This past Easter season, during one of our base Chaplain Corps luncheons, this potentially bad joke actually became a good news story. The visiting Chaplain Rabbi, who was on hand to provide

Passover services to our Jewish personnel joined two Chaplain Roman Catholic priests and several Chaplain Protestant ministers for lunch at the DFAC. The Rabbi (eating a Kosher Meal-Ready-to-Eat), the Catholic and Liturgical clergy (limiting themselves to some food items due to the observance of Lent) and other ministers, including Baptists (eating everything in sight!) gathered as if this was an everyday occurrence. Theologically, the differences in the room were immense. A man who was still awaiting the coming of the Messiah sat by a man who embraces the celebration of the risen Christ. He sat by a man who worships with loud choruses who sat by a man who finds meaning in contemplation who sat by a Calvinist who sat by an Armenian. No joke—just another meal at the DFAC. Now, understand, when men and women join the military chaplaincy, their beliefs are not thrown into some giant ecumenical/interfaith blender losing all religious and denominational distinctives. It is not uncommon for chaplains to informally gather and have friendly discussions about faith and doctrine. This lunch, however, was simply a time when chaplains, from a wide-range of theological spectrums, came together to say a prayer and share a meal during a seasonal convergence of religious observances. The group-unifier was the common uniform we wore and the constitutional mandate to provide or provide for the religious needs of the Airmen we serve.

We were certainly not the first or the last group of diverse military chaplains to fellowship and cooperate together. Chaplains have been part of the American military culture since the Revolutionary War. A hallmark story of interfaith chaplain ministry is the WWII account of the "Four Chaplains," also known as "The

Immortal Chaplains." On January 23, 1943 the converted 5,649 ton civilian cruise ship, *USAT Dorchester* left New York as part of a convoy of three vessels. They were cruising through icy waters from Newfoundland toward an American base in Greenland. The *Dorchester* was carrying approximately 902 passengers—merchant seaman, civilian workers, and soldiers—including four Army Chaplains. These four were relatively new Army officers, all holding the rank of Lieutenant. They included a Methodist minister, George Fox; a Rabbi, Alexander D. Goode; a Roman Catholic Priest, John P. Washington; and a Reformed Church minister, Clark V. Poling. Fox was the oldest at age 42, the others were in their early thirties.

At 12:55a.m. on February 3, 1943, the *Dorchester* was torpedoed by a German submarine 150 miles from its destination. The explosion disabled the vessel's electrical system, leaving the ship dark. Panic ensued as the *Dorchester* began to sink. The chaplains sought to calm the men and organize an orderly evacuation while helping the wounded to safety. In the process, they gave up their own lifejackets and assisted as many men as they could into the limited number of lifeboats. When giving up their lifejackets, Rabbi Goode did not call out for a Jew, Father Washington did not call out for a Catholic, Pastors Fox and Poling did not call out for a Protestant. Against the backdrop of incredible hardship and despair, the chaplains provided a steady voice and a calm reassurance to all. As the ship began to list, survivors saw the four chaplains with arms linked and braced upon the slanting deck. They were singing hymns and praying prayers. Some men reported hearing different languages mixed in the prayers of the chaplains, including Jewish prayers in Hebrew and Catholic prayers in Latin. Tragically, the four eventually went down with the ship, disappearing into the frigid waters of the North Atlantic. Of the 902 men aboard, 672 died, leaving 230 survivors. When news reached the American shores, the nation was stunned by the magnitude of the tragedy and the story of the extraordinary faith, courage, and selflessness of the four chaplains.

The story of the Four Chaplains has captured and held the imagination of people for over 70 years. It has been depicted in print, art, film, music and a two-hour audio documentary entitled "No Greater Love" A U.S. Postage stamp was created in their honor in 1948. In 1988, February 3rd was established by a unanimous act of Congress as an annual "Four Chaplains Day." Ceremonies and services are held each year on or around the February 3rd date by numerous military and civilian groups and organizations.

Two memorial foundations have been formed—one with the mission to "further the cause of 'unity without uniformity' by encouraging goodwill and cooperation among all people." What could appear at first glance to be a bad joke wrought with theological tension is instead a story of goodwill and cooperation centered around a common cause and shared sacrifice. Spread the word! Men and women from diverse theological backgrounds can actually work together without compromising their faith and practice! People who wear yarmulkes can minister alongside people who wear collars alongside people who wear robes alongside people who wear suits alongside people who wear Dockers. Let us never be afraid to work with "those people", even in theological circles. "Those people" are God's creations who have great value. "Those people" have dreams, aspirations, fears, and failures. In fact, from a Christian perspective, "those people" are located somewhere in the "Jerusalem, Judea, Samaria, or the uttermost" that we are commissioned to reach. Could it be that it is easier to dialogue and reach people in whom we are already joining hands in compassionate and cooperative efforts? In an ever-increasing divisive world, let us continue to find ways to further the cause of 'unity without uniformity'…and perhaps, as Jesus taught, "By this all men will know you are my disciples, if you love one another."

Next time you hear about a Rabbi, a Priest, and a Minister walking into a room, think of the possibilities. Don't laugh… it may be the start of something remarkably good!

Email 9—May 5, 2012

All,
Happy Cinco de Mayo! I found out that yesterday was "Star Wars Day" (May the 4th be with you!) Anyway, things are still rolling along here! May has brought some consistently hot temperatures (111 degrees as I write). The temperature will continue to rise through the summer!

I am attaching three pictures. The second gives a typical look at the base here. Lots of white rocks that reflect off the hot sun! The third picture is also at the base—it's a reminder that we are part of a coalition of forces. The remaining picture is one of myself, the chaplain I work with (yes, the guy on the right) and a leading military member of our host country. The picture was taken recently at a gathering that he invited us to attend—a sort of goodwill gesture. I don't take it lightly that I have the opportunity to not only rub shoulders with some incredible American Airmen, soldiers, sailors, and marines, but also Coalition members and other foreign nationals. Hopefully, we are all learning from each other!

Remember (especially guys!) that next Sunday is Mother's Day! Be sure to give her a call or hug. For those of us who no longer have our moms here on earth, it can be a time to reflect but a little sad as well. Last week, one of our base chaplain assistant's wife gave birth to their second son. Of course, the chaplain assistant was here, and his wife was back in Virginia—8000 miles away. He was able to "be with her" during the delivery thanks to his smart phone and Facetime! Facetime and Skype are remarkable technologies and are able to connect Service members in ways that, just a few years ago would have seemed unimaginable. Mom and baby are doing well.

Thanks for allowing me to share a few thoughts— keep pressing on and have a great week!

Randy

Email 10—May 16, 2012

Friends,

Hope all is well!

One of the benefits of this particular deployment is that we are able to go into town occasionally and enjoy the culture of Doha, Qatar. Today, I visited the Doha campus of Texas A&M! Yes, there are Aggies in Qatar!

It's one of seven American schools at the "Education

City" complex. You can read more about TAMU in Qatar at http://www.qatar.tamu.edu/. BTW, I learned that if you are a Texas resident, you can enroll at Texas A&M, Qatar at Texas tuition rates—pretty good deal! I saw some "Howdy" signs, or as they also say, "Al Salaam" (Ahl sah-LAHM).

This past Saturday and Sunday I had the opportunity to preach at four separate Worship services—2 Contemporary, 1 Traditional, and 1 Gospel. It reminded me of the myriad of expressions of Worship from God's people. The Traditional service incorporated responsive readings, the Apostle's Creed, and communion. The Contemporary Service included a Praise team and various instruments. The Gospel Service with even livelier music and lots of swaying was the most animated of all! In each I preached the same message, "Down By the Riverside" from Acts 16:10-15. The passage reminds us that God is guiding our paths and all of us being able to make a difference. Though the worship style differed, each service contained men and women willing to receive and apply the Word. At any rate, it was fun, I appreciated the opportunity.

Take care!

Randy

The months of May and June brought some brutally hot weather. Before I departed, the temperature rose to 118 degrees. That, coupled with the incessantly blowing wind made me praise the Lord for hardened structures and air conditioning, two items not available for all deployers.

Because of the heat, water bottles were plentiful. Pallets of plastic water bottles were in place throughout the complex. One of the noises I grew to hate was the crushing of the plastic water bottles when the bottle was empty. I understand the purpose.

Crushing the bottle conserves space in the trash. But the sound was everywhere and every day. I heard it in the large outdoor gathering area, I heard it in the DFAC, I heard it in meeting rooms, and yes, I heard it resound in the large CAOC. Smash, smash, crush, crush.

I made the mistake in telling one of our chaplain assistants how much that noise was grating on my nerves. It was a private conversation. The next day, someone across the room, I think someone across in the PA office, with a smile on his face, called out, "hey chaplain!" The sound of a crushing plastic water bottle ensued. Maybe a bit of TV channel-changing-revenge? I forced a smile and gave a nod of approval. I have heard that all is fair in love and war—certainly, this CAOC encounter was a combination of the two!

The date of my end of tour was approaching. The new team was beginning to arrive to fill new positions for the next six months, including mine. I felt fortunate to serve with and alongside dedicated Airmen for the past six months. Though I was ready to get back home, leaving this place and these people was bittersweet. Friendships had been formed and circumstances had forged our relationships. Soon, I would board a plane and eventually get back to Texas. For the first time in a long time, I would also unemployed! More to come on that!

Email 11—July 4, 2012

All,

Happy Fourth of July! If you are Facebook "Friends" with Susie on Facebook, you know that my deployment is complete and I'm back in Dallas. As you know, she has been chronicling my return with a daily and hourly update! By far, the past six months have been tougher on her than me—she has been a real trooper throughout.

Last Wednesday, I left Qatar to Baltimore, with stops in Italy and Germany—the trip took about 18 hours. When traveling on a military "rotator", we are required to wear our military uniforms. After arriving in Baltimore, thoroughly worn out and ready to spend the night for the next leg of the journey. I walked through the airport to catch a shuttle to the hotel. Still inside, almost to the baggage claim, I rounded a corner and heard some cheers. With a sudden lump in my throat, myself and fellow military members were welcomed back home. The great people of Baltimore, I'm guessing over 100 were gathered, ranging from children to senior adults, had lined up with banners, streamers, and cheers to welcome a group of anonymous service members. Though I have seen this several times on T.V., to be in the middle of it put a lump in my throat and tears to my eyes.

I wanted to say "thanks" to each of you as well, because you were part of the celebration. Thanks for your prayers, notes of encouragement, and continued friendship. You stood by with streamers and cheers throughout. Your presence was daily felt and much appreciated. The fact is, we are all part of a great adventure—my prayers are with you as you journey ahead. We don't know what is around the corner, but we are assured of God's presence. Keep pressing on toward the path He leads! As the writer of Hebrews reminds us, we have a "great cloud of witnesses" cheering and inspiring us along the way!

I'm not quite sure what is in store for the Marshalls, we are discerning His next step for us. I appreciate your continued prayers for the next place of ministry while I continue serving part-time in the Air Force Reserve.

Again, Happy 4th! Together, lets celebrate our national freedoms as we gratefully reflect upon those Servicemembers, Statesmen, and Citizens who have and continue to pave the way.

Randy

IN THE MEANTIME

"Humble yourselves, therefore, under God's mighty hand, that He may lift you up in due time. "Cast your anxiety on Him because He cares for you." James 5:6-7

It was great to be back in Texas and back home with Susie. Vocationally, there was some uncertainty. With the Air Force, I returned to a part-time Reserve (IMA) status. I was able to complete a two-week tour (back at SOUTHCOM,) but was unable to perform any additional days due to the 1095 ceiling. The months from July 2012 to June 2013 are somewhat a blur. Promising ministry opportunities failed to materialize. Denominational and Pastor positions were slow in developing. I once more reflected on the story of Noah. Like Noah, I was on a floating barge with no real destination. I believe the boat I traveled was called, "Patience." I had daily talks with God about this. Finally, I prayed, "Lord, I know that you are trying to teach me patience in knowing and discerning your will. After a lot of thought, I believe my lesson is done. I am now patient. Lord, please show me your direction…now!" I think I heard God laugh. In the next few months, I worked for Marketplace Ministries, an industrial chaplain ministry based out of Plano. It was and is a tremendous ministry to impact businesses, but I knew it wasn't the long-term solution.

I would say many times I believe I have enough faith that if

God sent me a fax, email, personal letter, burning bush, whatever…and He clearly gave me guidance, I would follow. But, on this portion of the journey, there was nothing on the horizon. Like Noah, this tour of duty had no end date. The one thing that brought hope to the basic trainee at Lackland and the deployer in the field was the end of tour date. No date had been set, no end to the journey of "Patience" was known.

In late 2012 and early 2013, opportunities suddenly became abundant. I was being considered by a church in the Dallas/Ft. Worth area that was seeking a senior pastor. There was an opening for an administrator at a Baptist Encampment. I was being considered for another denominational position. There were also military options.

I had recently pinned on Colonel. On an Active-Duty military base, pinning on a new rank is highly celebrated with a ceremony surrounded by coworkers, family and friends. For a reservist, particularly an IMA that lives far from a local base, putting on the new rank means you go to the Base Exchange, pick it up, and wear it next time you serve! Anyway, at this level, I had applied to attend the military in-residence school, "Air War College." Air War College is a highly competitive year-long school for Air Force Lt Colonels and Colonels held at Maxwell AFB in Montgomery, Alabama. Because the competition is against "Line Officers," it is very rare for a Reserve Air Force chaplain to be chosen. In fact, at that time, only two had ever been selected. I received notice in the Fall that I was chosen to be an alternate. Early in 2013, I was informed that there was a cancellation and now I was on the primary list. Now, I was in a quandary. If I accepted, it was a tremendous honor, but it would also mean that in one year I would be back in the same position of uncertainty. Or, should I wait and see if the other opportunities, especially the pastor position, pans out?

Though I did not receive a fax, email, letter, or burning bush as a sign, I accepted the Air War College offer. Susie and I were preparing for another move when in early June something totally unexpected happened. I had also applied to be the Deputy Command Chaplain at the U.S. Reserve Command, a position located in Warner Robins, GA. Historically, the Deputy Command Chaplain eventually moved up to the Command Chaplain position. Each of these positions were a total of 3 years with a chance to extend. (1095 rules did not apply to these types of orders.) I had applied with very little expectation. These full-time Air Guard Reserve (AGR) positions were few and far between. I didn't think I was "in the loop" to be considered. One other candidate seemed to be on the short list.

One day, in perusing my emails on my phone, in my parked car, I saw an email from the Reserve Personnel Center in Denver, Colorado. I expected it to say something like "thanks for applying, but…" To my surprise, it indicated that indeed, I had been selected. I turned to Susie, who was in the passenger seat and said, "you are not going to believe this…" I then called the Air Force Reserve Chaplain's office and let them know that I have received the email and would be accepting the position. I then asked, "what about Air War College?" Not to worry, those orders would be rescinded. Looks like all signs were pointing to military, just not the position I had anticipated.

This journey taught me that in navigating God's Will, I must maintain trust. Though I was able to readjust my military plans, if I had been offered and accepted any of the full-time ministry opportunities, I would have had to decline the AGR position. Surprise! God actually knew what He was doing! He knew this assignment was in the works. The wait, though painstaking, was well worth it. Though there were still steps to be taken, God provided a leaf, a leaf of hope and promise. I was about to disembark from this seemingly aimless floating emotion-filled barge. The journey was set to continue with a new and exciting course.

Using my group email from the deployment, I sent the following email:

JUNE 18, 2013

All,

I wanted to give you a quick update on the Marshalls. I was notified last week that I have been selected as the Deputy Command Chaplain at the Air Force Reserve Command at Robins AFB in Warner Robins, Georgia. It is a three-year (full-time) tour. The position is a tremendous opportunity of influence and ministry to and with the AF Reserve. After my deployment last year, my intent was to come back and stay in Texas—the Lord had other plans!

So, after the wedding in Denver next week (Blake and Lindsey), Susie and I will be headed to Georgia. I report on July 12th. I will send another email and will include our contact info. The invitation is open to all to come visit. (Of course, if you all come at the same time, some of you will be sleeping outside!)

Thanks again for all of your love and support as we

take another leg of the Great Adventure! My prayers are
with you in your journey as well.
Take care,
Randy

Randy Marshall

Air Force Reserve Command Headquarters
2013

Randy Marshall

Air Force Reserve Command Deputy Command Chaplain

For most of my Air Force career, the work of the Air Force Reserve Command (AFRC) Headquarters was a mystery. In my sixteen years at Randolph and Lackland and special tours at Nellis and the Air Force Academy, I was supervised directly by local senior chaplains. I focused on the mission at these particular locations. As an IMA, working at Active-Duty locations, I rarely came across other reservists. Though I was aware of the function and purpose of the Reserve Command, it was just background music as I ministered at the local level. That awareness changed when I worked the Patriot Defender exercise. During that time, my "base of attachment" was at Robins AFB, the location of the Air Force Command Headquarters. As an IMA, I spent some time at the Chaplain's office and became immersed with its mission and purpose.

Now, I am arriving to be one of its senior leaders. Unlike most bases I served, I was now surrounded by fellow reservists. In the Chaplain's office, it consisted of thirteen staff.—seven AGR chaplains, two AGR enlisted (chaplain assistants), two Active-Duty chaplains (also called "Regular Air Force") one Active Duty chaplain assistant, and two civilians. The Command Chaplain, Ch, Col Gary Califf was one of the AGRs. Aside from a deployed location, having a senior chaplain at the base or command level as a Reserve chaplain did not fit the Air Force Command structure— except for the Reserve Command. At the time, the only AGR Chaplain Corps positions available were at Robins. So, I felt incredibly blessed to not only be on the staff but hold one of the two Colonel positions.

The office was responsible for all Reserve Chaplain Corps members across the United States and the World—over 480 personnel. The two divisions within the office, Personnel and Plans/Program Divisions, kept continual contact with the IMAs and TRs as they provided spiritual care and religious advisement to their bases. The Command Chaplain's office had four "Key Processes":

1. Advise Leadership
2. Oversee Resources
3. Interpret/Implement Policies
4. Execute Processes

This was done with the backdrop of the AFRC overall mission to provide a combat-ready Chaplain Corps—ready spiritually, emotionally, mentally, and physically to meet the task at hand. In many ways, this task was much more complex than their civilian minister counterparts.

Concerning personnel, it was important for the Chaplain Corps member to be at the right place at the right time. This benefited both the member and the base of assignment. When it was apparent the member had been at a location for a period of time, they were encouraged to move to another base. I received such a call when I pinned on Major and was encouraged to move from Lackland to Randolph for my personal growth and "Force Development." An interesting dynamic in this process is that a reserve Air Force member can decline the opportunity to move. This is a "head scratcher" to the Active-Duty world where moves are not voluntary. Saying "no" to an assignment from higher headquarters means you are no longer part of the Air Force. The Air Force Reserve recognizes that these military members are also civilians with civilian jobs. Saying "no" could limit future military opportunities and hinder future promotions, but personal and civilian professional considerations were honored.

Two major responsibilities of the Plans/Programs Division were recruiting and the planning and implementation of the Chaplain Candidate Program—a training for seminarians who have received an Air Force commission on how to become a chaplain. This included an additional 100 personnel to manage.

The role of the Deputy Command Chaplain was to ensure these roles were performed smoothly and efficiently. The role was central in securing funding through the appropriate AFRC channels. It also included travel to various locations. The Command Chaplain oversaw the entire process while being ultimately responsible to the Air Force Reserve three-star commander.

The Chaplain's office was one of several offices throughout the command. Picture the multi-disciplinary atmosphere of the deployed CAOC and expand it with various personnel, spread throughout several building at Robins. Each worked in their particular field of expertise while serving under the same command. Of course, as with most organizations, this involved several ongoing meetings.

The stated mission of the Air Force Reserve Command is to "provide combat ready forces to fly, fight, and win." The Command, one of nine major commands provides about 14 percent of the Total Force mission. IMAs provide a "backfill" function to the Active Duty. TRs directly support "nuclear deterrence operations, air, space and cyberspace superiority, command and control, global integrated intelligence surveillance reconnaissance, global precision attack, special operations, rapid global mobility and personnel recovery. They also perform space operations, aircraft flight testing, aerial port operations, civil engineer, security forces, military training, communications, mobility support, transportation and services missions.[1]

Over 70,000 Airmen serve, in various statuses, with various jobs, throughout the United States and deployed locations across the world. Then and now, the Chaplain Corps is ready and available to provide spiritual care and religious advisement.

NEW BEGINNING

So once again, I was starting anew—new people to meet, new systems to learn, new challenges and new opportunities. I immediately learned a lesson on the first day. My new office space was somewhat bare—it contained a metal desk, file cabinet, and a small table. I also noted some dust on the floor. So, as I was getting settled in, I asked one of the chaplain assistants if we had a vacuum cleaner. Honestly, it was an innocent question. I simply wanted to vacuum the floor of my office before I started moving in. After asking the question, I went around the corner to speak with the administrative assistant. Within minutes, I returned to my office. I was taken aback. In the office were three chaplain assistants vacuuming my office and dusting my desk and cabinet. One began to profusely apologize. The question had taken a direction I had not anticipated. When I asked for a vacuum, it was Randy asking for a vacuum cleaner. What they heard was Chaplain, Colonel Randy Marshall, the Deputy Command Chaplain cryptically say, "someone needs to vacuum this carpet!"

Over the years, I would recount this story often. It is a great example of how rank can make our voices louder than we intend. Over the years, some deep relationships were formed with both chaplains and chaplain assistants. I wanted to create a work environment where the mission at hand was accomplished, while at the same time doing work that was meaningful and fulfilling. It also included some good-natured ribbing. I told a joke one day and one of my chaplain assistants laughed. It was obviously a fake laugh. As he did, he rubbed his collar mirroring where my Colonel Eagle rank was located. I got the meaning. He was "laughing" because the Colonel told the joke and he felt required to laugh! After that, whenever I would say something that brought some laughter to this Airman, I would ask him, "was that really funny or was it Colonel funny?"

PERRY

Robins AFB is located in Warner Robins, Georgia, just south

of Macon. When looking for homes, we looked around Warner Robins and throughout Houston County. Allow me to diverge. I took issue with the name "Houston." In Texas, the name "Houston" is pronounced "hew-ston. The Georgia pronunciation of the word, "Houston" is "House-ton". Now, any good Texan knows how to pronounce one of the largest cities in Texas. It didn't seem right that a state could just change the pronunciation. Warner Robins even had a "Houston" street. I was encouraged to hear the voice on my phone GPS pronounce it correctly. Apparently, the mispronunciation of the word has been going on since 1821. One of the first Governors of Georgia was John Houstoun. Somewhere along the way, the spelling was changed and the letter u was omitted. As much as I tried to reason with the residents, they never relented. I did note that there was also a city in Georgia called "Dallas" in which they pronounced correctly. I quipped that if they were going to be consistent, they should call the town, "Dollas."

Another oddity that I noticed in this part of Georgia is their geographical name. In Texas, the center of the state is called "Central Texas." In Georgia, the center of the state is called, "Middle Georgia." I always thought it sounded very Tolkien.

Anyway, here we were in Middle Georgia, in Houston County looking for a suitable home. We finally settled in Perry, a town around 14 miles southwest of the base. Perry is the county seat of Houston County. Though it was a bit of a daily commute, it was worth the drive. Susie and I had spent the last four years in the metropolitan areas of Miami and Dallas. We were ready to get back to small-town life. Though Warner Robins could be considered a small town (approximate population: 81,000), Perry was much smaller (approximate population: 22.000.) Perry also had a very distinctive and quaint downtown area. We also found a church, the First Baptist Church in Perry, that we felt very much at home. It was a church where friendships were made, and I was regularly given opportunities to preach and lead small group Bible Studies.

The house we chose was a new construction that had been built in the middle of a pecan orchard. Our relatively small lot contained five trees that produced many pounds of pecans. The United States is the world's leading producer of pecans and Georgia is historically the leading pecan-producing State. A typical pecan crop is around 72 million pounds. My five trees were part of the mix!

MORE ON THE CHAPLAIN CANDIDATE PROGRAM

There are two distinct paths in becoming an Air Force Chaplain. The first is a direct appointment. A direct appoint chaplain is an United States Citizen who has completed all required education including a baccalaureate degree with no less than 120 semester hours of credit from an accredited college or university, has completed a Master's Degree in Theology from an accredited institution, possesses an ecclesiastical endorsement from a recognized denomination or faith group (normally requiring a certain number of years of pastoral experience) and be spiritually, morally, intellectually, and emotionally sound to serve Air Force personnel. Because all of these conditions must be met, a direct appoint chaplain enters military service a bit later than those of equal rank. This is the path I took. Upon approval, the minister becomes a chaplain with the rank of First Lieutenant. All Airmen wear some sort of occupational badge on their uniform to distinguish their job. As previously noted, the chaplain's occupational badge is also an ecclesiastical symbol. For an overwhelming number, the symbol on a chaplain is a cross indicating a Christian chaplain. The same symbol represents both Catholic and various protestant denominations. Other chaplain religious symbols include: tablets for a Jewish chaplain, an eight-spoked wheel for Buddhist chaplains, and an Islamic Crescent for Muslim chaplains.

The second path to becoming an Air Force Chaplain is through the Chaplain Candidate Program. This program is designed for the seminarian who has an interest in Air Force Chaplaincy. Before his/her actual seminary degree and before ecclesiastical endorsement, the student (who has ecclesiastical approval) enters into this program. Upon approval, the student goes through Officer Training School (in the summer months) to become an Air Force Officer. He/She receives the rank of Second Lieutenant. Since a Chaplain Candidate is still in training, he/she does not wear a religious badge.

The Air Force Reserve Chaplain's Office has responsibility to train seminarians in the Chaplain Candidate Program. This is a Total Force training for all interested in Air Force Chaplaincy—Active Duty, Reserve and National Guard. It involves much coordination and a tremendous amount of resources including adding additional manpower to augment training. The annual summer focus is the Chaplain Candidate Intensive Internship (CCII). When spoken, this acronym is pronounced, "C2I2."

CCII is a 35-day course that covers eight military installations in five states. It has one mission, to train the next generation of Air

Force Chaplains. It is, what we described a "look and see" program that hopefully opened the eyes of the seminarians to what Chaplaincy is all about. There is no long-term commitment. The program is a combination of instruction and practical application. Their travel, primarily by military transport, took them to different locations to see and experience various mission sets. These missions included training environments, combat operations, Special Forces operations, and a variety of others based on availability. The Candidates observed flight-line ministry, chapel ministry, and scenarios where they felt the stress of combat ministry. With the guidance of Chaplain Corps mentors, they were continuously exposed to various environments and then given the ability to debrief and learn even more.

As Deputy Command Chaplain, I would periodically travel to these bases and check on the progress of the training. Engaging with these Seminarians was one of my highlights of the year. They were eager to learn and willing to stretch their limits as they discerned their calling in this diverse and pluralistic environment.

For Chaplain Candidates in their second and third year of the program, they would individually spend 30 days at an assigned base to be mentored and receive more training. Their final step before becoming a chaplain after all ecclesiastical and educational requirements had been met, is the interview led by the Deputy Command Chaplain. It was here that myself and two other staff chaplains would ask a series of questions including their sense of calling to become a chaplain, the reality of ministering in a pluralistic environment, challenges they have faced, etc…Unless some major red flags were raised, they were then presented to a formal board led by the Command Chaplain to accept or reject the candidate. If accepted, our office coordinated his/her initial assignment. (A disclaimer to the reader—some of the details of the program have changed, but the focus to train future chaplains remains.)

This was just one area of our office's responsibility. During my three years as Deputy Command Chaplain, I had multiple engagements with IMAs and TRs at their bases throughout the United States. I attended multiple briefings. I was involved in looking at our processes and leading the team in process improvement.

Much of what I did was administrative. Years ago, there was a company named BASF whose tagline was "At BASF, we don't make a lot of the products you buy. We make a lot of the products you buy better."[2] That is how I felt most days. Our office was constantly advocating for more resources and providing training so that the local chaplains and chaplain assistants could be fully equipped. Of course, I also had the opportunity to encourage our staff on a daily basis and provide ministry to AFRC personnel. I provided invocations for a variety of ceremonies, conducted religious engagement in work centers and was available when someone approached me and said, "chaplain, I need to talk."

Toward the end of my Deputy Command Chaplain tour, I also took an Interim Pastor Position at Shirley Hills Baptist Church in Warner Robins. I had truly missed being in the pulpit to preach and teach. Since I did not have any Sunday responsibilities and the majority of my travel was during the week, I was able to fulfill this role. While the Pastor Search Committee was looking for their next pastor, I filled in the best I could. During my time in Georgia, I served as Interim pastor at three churches—Shirley Hills Baptist Church, First Baptist Church in Warner Robins, and First Baptist Church in Marshallville (yes, Marshallville!) At each church, I was able to preach God's Word, encourage them during the interim period, and always, always remind them that the proper pronunciation of the word "Houston!"

EDIMGIAFAD

If you happen to drive to Warner Robins, you will see an acronym throughout town—EDIMGIAFAD. On Watson Boulevard, in front of businesses, cut into the shrubbery, EDIMGIAFAD. On the side of buildings and on the water tower, EDIMGIAFAD. Visitors and newcomers to town will see this acronym and eventually ask, "what in the world does that mean." It then gives the opportunity for a citizen of Warner Robins to answer, "Every Day In Middle Georgia Is Armed Forces Appreciation Day." This acronym was a gentle reminder to military members and their families that their presence was noticed and appreciated.

The acronym has roots that go back to the 1960s, in an unfortunate time in our nation's history. In 1968, at the height of the Vietnam War, military members were spat upon and disrespected when they returned home. A local physician, Dr. Dan Callahan wanted to do something to honor these men and women. EDIMGIAFAD was born. Businesses started putting it on their signs, letterheads, business cards, and yes, shrubbery. The acronym originally meant, "Every Day In Middle Georgia is Air Force Appreciation Day." As the base continued to take on more missions, Callahan and other local leaders thought it would be better to change "Air Force" to the more encompassing, "Armed Forces."

Interest in the acronym has expanded beyond Georgia. A complementary saying has been developed for use throughout the United States—EDIUSAIAFAD meaning, "Every Day in the United States of America is Armed Forces Appreciation Day." This acronym is longer and even harder to pronounce. The intent is the same—recognizing and having a thankful attitude to our nation's military.[3]

I have been fortunate to live in a time of intense national pride in our men and women in military service. It was common for me to walk into a grocery store while in uniform and hear the words, "thank you for your service." In churches I pastored in Texas and the interim pastorates in Georgia, recognizing Veterans on Sundays close to Veterans Day had been a highlight. On these Sundays, I wore my uniform, inviting Veterans to do the same. The services recognized our Veterans and Servicemembers while giving all glory to God. Sundays surrounding Memorial Day and Independence Day also prayerfully acknowledged the sacrifice of those who served. Words cannot express what community and national support means to military members and their families, not only during days focused on patriotism and remembrance, but every day.

To our grateful nation, EDIMGIAFAD or EDIUSAAFAD, no matter how you spell or say it—military members, past and present, salute you and thank you for your support!

Randy Marshall

Air Force Reserve Command

2017

Randy Marshall

Command Chaplain

Upon Ch Califf's retirement, I was selected as the Command Chaplain. This was my last and most fulfilling role in the Air Force.

In order to help us communicate with personnel throughout the Command, AFRC Staff Chaplains would write a "Good Word" to be distributed to those who had requested these types of emails. Though I wrote the article below a year prior in 2016, it reflects on the change of leadership and my sentiments in this new assignment.

"Ready or not, a new year has arrived! Like previous years, throughout 2016 we will experience ups, downs, highs and lows…all with a wide variety of corresponding emotions in rhythm with the ebb and flow of daily life. Though we can anticipate rich, enjoyable moments, we are also well-aware that our days can be quickly interrupted by an unwanted assault on our well-thought-out dreams and seemingly perfect plans. Though we have every reason to approach the new year with hopeful anticipation, we can, especially in these uncertain times, have overwhelming feelings of out-of-control fear and dread in what lies ahead. As we journey into 2016, consider the words of Joshua 1:9, "Have I not commanded you? Be strong and courageous. Do not be afraid; do not be discouraged for the Lord your God will be with you wherever you go." In Joshua 1, the words, "be strong and courageous" are stated three times by God to the newly chosen leader, Joshua. Later in the chapter, Joshua relays the same charge, "be strong and courageous" to the people he was about to lead. Much like entering into a new year, the people of Israel were at the precipice of entering new ground, filled with giant-sized challenges. Though there would be joyful moments ahead, there would also be times of testing and uncertainty. Both the leader and the people needed to heed the call to be strong and courageous. This direct command was followed by a corresponding promise…" for the Lord your God will be with you wherever you go." The reason they (and we) could even consider possessing strength and courage to face the day was (and is) because of the mighty presence of our God.

We don't know what the future holds, but we know Who holds the future—as we enter the new year, be strong and courageous, let us confidently face the opportunities and challenges ahead—with the calm, blessed assurance that God is with us wherever we go."

PLAYER COACH

What do sports figures Bill Russell, Lenny Wilkens, Ernie Nevers, Curly Lambeau, George Halas, and Tom Landry have in common? They were all, at one time, Player-Coaches. They had a coaching position while also being an active player. Though common at one time, for a variety of reasons, a Player-Coach is no longer a possibility in professional sports…at least to my knowledge. In a rank-dominated structure of the U.S. Military, one may assume there is a top-down approach to making things happen. It is true that sometimes orders are given with no ability to debate.

For example, if during a battle, the Army Sergeant gives an order to "charge the hill!", men under his command charge the hill. There is no additional conversation. There is no response like, "Yeah, I really don't think so..." or, "Let's think this over a bit..."

In an office environment, like the Chaplain's Office, it is wise to have a Player-Coach mentality. Some things are absolutes. Like a flowing mountain stream, it was important to stay within the banks—the priorities of the AFRC Commander, functional priorities of the Air Force Chief of Chaplains, responsibilities spelled out in the Air Force Instructions (AFIs) and making sure everything is legal. Within those banks are decisions to be made—personnel decisions, process improvement decisions, unit engagement decisions, etc...There were many times I would gather my senior Chaplain Corps staff and hash out these things. I would encourage an exchange of ideas to hopefully enhance the decision-making process. Sometimes that exchange would open a new understanding and the direction I thought we should go was adjusted or totally changed. A couple of times, I actually went against their advice. They knew and I knew that all AFRC Chaplain Corps decisions were ultimately decided by the Command Chaplain. But, the staff also knew that their perspective was valued and appreciated.

In order to have that kind of cooperative collaboration, being surrounded by the right staff was essential. The senior staff consisted of the Deputy Command Chaplain (Colonel), the two Division Chiefs (Lt Colonels), and the Senior Enlisted Chaplain Assistant (Chief Master Sergeant.) All but the Deputy Command Chaplain were already on board when I took the position. I had a history with each. The newly chosen Deputy Command Chaplain, Ch Towery, had previously led our Chaplain Candidate mentors (cadre) on a CCII tour. The two Division Chiefs, Ch Seaman and Ch Danford were two students of mine at a Patriot Defender training ten years prior. The Senior Chaplain Assistant, Chief Gray had worked years in the office, and as an IMA had assisted me several times with my military orders.

So, my stint as Command Chaplain had begun, the game was on. As Player-Coach I wanted to move the ball forward without fumbling it along the way!

For the next three and a half years, the staff activities that were done in my time as Deputy continued. Our recruiters continued to recruit. The Chaplain Candidate program continued to flourish. Conferences and training events were held. Chief Gray and I had several site-visits to various TR units. I participated on Promotion boards at the Air Reserve Personnel Center in Denver. Annually, members of our staff traveled to Denver to "vector" our chaplains and chaplain assistants for future assignments and professional development. I also traveled to the Pentagon in Washington D.C. to communicate and coordinate with the Chief of Chaplains office. The Chief of Chaplains was Ch Dondi Costin. Yes, this was the same Dondi Costin that I knew as a Captain at Lackland, as a Lt Col at the Air Force Chaplaincy school, and as a Colonel at Al Udeid. Now he was serving as the Major General (two-star) Chief of Chaplains. One of the joys of coming to this point in my career was seeing people I knew from long ago and being able to ask, "remember when?"

Though the work at Robins was serious, I attempted to make

the days enjoyable. The Chaplain's office should be the most fun, right?! We had some animals show up that helped keep us on track during our weekly AFRC Chaplain Corps staff meetings—stuffed animals that is. On the shelf was a stuffed squirrel. If it was perceived that someone had gone off track from the discussion, someone would say, "squirrel!" and throw it on the table. We also had a stuffed rabbit (chasing a rabbit) was used in the same way. Additionally on the shelf was a stuffed horse. When we determined that an idea had run its course or if was legacy (outdated) thinking, we would present the horse and use a well-worn axiom, "When the horse is dead, it is time to dismount!" We also had an Elmo doll. If someone had exhausted the conversation I may announce, "ELMO" meaning, "Enough, let's move on!" Another phrase we may use is "the good idea fairy." Though we didn't have a doll, it would identify an idea that was not feasible or was outside our Chaplain Corps "lane." I could say more, but I will invoke—ELMO— Enough, let's move on!"

Our Chaplain Corps staff had occasional off-sites for planning. We also had Christmas parties in homes, complete with ugly Christmas sweaters. Events like this allowed us to meet spouses and children of our staff. We had birthday celebrations at the office, as well as celebrations of promotions and awards. Some on the staff would play an occasional golf game or basketball game. We would all participate in team-building events. The staff was more than just a group of employees, they were dedicated men and women who chose to serve their country in this environment. We were part of the great endeavor of Chaplain ministry. We worked hard, took time to know one another in and out of the office, and we continually shared and prayed for personal needs. In many ways, we were family.

AIR FORCE RESERVE COMMANDERS

As the Command Chaplain, I had a much greater access to the AFRC Senior leadership. During my stint, I served under two Air Force Reserve Commanders—Lt General Maryanne Miller, and Lt General Richard Scobee. The Air Force Reserve Commander actually wears two hats. Follow with me…The Air Force Reserve Commander is the Commander of the Air Force Reserve Command and also Commander of the Air Force Reserve. The Air Force Reserve is both a Command and a Component (like the Air Guard.) It is an important distinction because it gave the commander a direct connection to both Congress and the Air Force at large.

Gen Miller was a devout Catholic and would often tell stories of her interaction with Mother Teresa and the Sisters of Charity. She requested, and of course, we provided a chaplain to pray with her each morning before the duty day when she was in town. She later took an assignment to be the Commander of the Air Mobility Command, which was a huge honor.

The Command was then handed over to General Scobee. I had first met General Scobee at the Air Force Reserve "10th Headquarters," in Ft Worth, Texas, where he was the 10th AF Commander. He then became the Deputy Commander of the Reserve Command and now Commander of the Air Force Reserve. He was a huge supporter of Chaplain activities. In Ft Worth, he funded a special training for all 10th Air Force Chaplain Corps teams. He saw the value of chaplain teams ministering to the

Airmen and the ability to have chaplains available during times of mental, physical, emotional, and spiritual stress and fatigue. This priority extended to his position as the Air Force Reserve (AFR) Commander. Under his leadership, I was invited to command-level conferences. I gave thirty-minute briefings at the conferences speaking of the value of the Chaplain Corps and how commanders could utilize Chaplain Corps assets to assist their Airmen. An ongoing request that continued to emerge was the need for full-time Chaplain Corps members (AGRs) at select bases who had members on full-time status. These stand-alone bases were vulnerable because they lacked the ability to properly respond to emergency situations during non-Unit Training Assemblies. Our office was able to coordinate the efforts through the command structure. The mechanism was in motion and my Command Chaplain successor was able to see its fruition. Driven by Gen Scobee's leadership and Chaplain Corps advocacy, AGR Chaplain teams—chaplains and chaplain assistants were able to be funded and utilized.

Because of their dual status, AFR Commanders split their time between two locations—Warner Robins, Georgia and Washington D.C. Most commanders lived in Washington D.C. where they had a separate Air Force Reserve staff at the Pentagon to further advocate and communicate AFR needs and capabilities. At AFRC, in Warner Robins, the day-to-day operations were under the supervision of the Deputy Commander. During the majority of my time as Command Chaplain, this was Major General "Jay" Flournoy. Gen Flournoy was also extremely supportive of chaplains. He requested that I come to his office once a week before the duty day to say a prayer. This prayer involved personal needs that we discussed as well as command-level concerns. It certainly was humbling and a distinct honor to be able to pray with leaders as they made significant decisions on a daily basis.

TRAVEL

In my roles of both Deputy Command Chaplain and Command Chaplain, I frequently traveled. As mentioned, I traveled to training events, to Active-Duty bases and reserve bases, to the Pentagon in Washington D.C., to various AFRC and Active-Duty Conferences, and to Promotion boards and Developmental Boards at the Air Reserve Personnel Center(ARPC) in Denver, CO.

Usually, I traveled with CMSgt Gray and/or other members of the staff. Travel can be enjoyable but with security measures, dropped flights, and late nights, it can take its toll. Traveling as a military member can be mind-numbing. Picture this, on one trip, I drove from my home in Perry to the Atlanta Airport utilizing my Florida Sunpass on the Georgia HOV lane. I then boarded the plane and took a flight to Connecticut. When I arrived at the airport in Connecticut, I presented the rental car agent my Texas Driver's License that showed my Georgia address in order to rent a car with North Carolina license plates so that I could drive to Massachusetts!

On one trip, Susie accompanied me. The trip was a Major Command (MAJCOM) senior Religious Support Team (RST) conference at Hickam AFB in Honolulu, Hawaii. When I told Susie I was going to Hawaii, she calmly said, "you mean "we" are going to Hawaii." Yes, I mean "we." The conference lasted three days. Some of the participants, including Chief Gray, were planning to take leave and stay a few more days. Susie and I were not able to stay because I had a follow-up tour of duty. I was scheduled to lead an Air Force Chaplain Corps developmental team at ARPC in Denver on the following Monday. So, on this trip, we traveled from middle Georgia to California, to Honolulu, to Denver. When I lamented that I was not able to stay and see more of the beaches of Hawaii because I had to fly to the majestic mountains of Denver, strangely, no one took pity on me!

COMMANDER'S BRIEFING

As previously noted, commanders are found at various levels in the military organization. Each month, at AFRC/HC a briefing was provided for men and women, normally Majors and Lt Colonels, who were moving into command leadership positions. In these positions, it was important they knew base resources that were available. One of these resources in the commander's "toolkit" is the Chaplain Corps. Chaplains and chaplain assistants (name was later changed to Religious Affairs Airmen) were assigned to base locations. The commanders were very cognizant of the Chaplain Corps in the area of spiritual care—worship, unit engagement, counseling, etc…They were somewhat aware of the other core competency of the Chaplain Corps—religious advisement.

CMSgt Gray and I would provide the briefing. We would begin with a quote from Gen George C. Marshall: "The soldier's heart, the soldier's spirit, the soldier's soul, are everything. Unless the soldier's soul sustains him, he cannot be relied on and will fail himself and his commander and his country in the end."4

Change the word, "soldier" to "Airmen" and change pronouns to "he and she," you have a powerful message for today's Air Force. As a team, Chief Gray and I would then present the unique availability and contribution of their local Chaplain Corps presence.

Chief Gray would explain the value of chaplain assistants and how the chaplain and chaplain assistant formed a Religious Support Team (RST.) When entering a unit, the chaplain assistant would be the eyes and ears of the chaplain. Since a chaplain was an officer, the enlisted chaplain assistant could help bridge the gap in the conversation.

In this three-day course, the participants heard briefing after briefing from various AFRC offices. Instead of boring the group with another PowerPoint presentation, I designed a learning exercise I called "Deal or no Deal!" I gave a series of situations and asked the question, "deal or no deal?" and asked the participants to vote with a thumbs up or thumbs down. Reader, see how you do!

Question One: "A member has a Bible on his/her desk. Another co-worker complains. The supervisor immediately makes the member put the Bible in his desk drawer. Is this the appropriate response? Did the supervisor make the right decision?"

Thumbs up or thumbs down? Deal or no deal? Usually, the response was mixed. From each group, I asked why they voted the way they did, and a discussion ensued. Finally, I would provide the answer.

Answer: No Deal

Explanation: Since the Bible (or Koran or any other religious material) was in the member's personal space, based on his/her First Amendment Constitutional rights, the Airman was very much allowed to have the Bible for personal use. This should have been explained to the offended party.

Depending on the discussion, I would oftentimes have a follow-up question.

Question: "Instead of being on the desk of one of your staff, what if the Bible was on your desk (as commander.) Is this allowable?"

Answer: Deal

Explanation: Commanders have the same rights as any other Airman.

To make a final point, I would ask, "what if the Bible was a large family Bible perched on an easel?" This would be a "no deal" because now it has become a display instead of an item for personal use.

Question: "Should the commander allow the wear of religious apparel while in uniform?"

Answer: Sometimes Deal, sometimes No Deal.

Explanation: The commander may allow practice of a belief as long as it does not have an adverse impact on military readiness, unit cohesion, standards, or discipline. For example, Jewish personnel can wear a yarmulke (head covering) during a normal workday. They cannot wear it on the flightline where no hats are allowed due to safety reasons.

Question: "You (the commander) and your spouse have a new baby that will be baptized at the Catholic Church next Sunday. You invite those who live in the area to attend."

Answer: "Deal" within reason.

Explanation: It is not wrong in itself to invite; however, it must be acknowledged that the commander's voice holds a lot of weight. It is here that I would share my vacuum story on my first day as Deputy Command Chaplain. What is stated or requested may not be what is heard. Commanders, like all military members, have no obligation to hide their religious faith. However, commanders must be careful, whether real or perceived, to avoid coercion of a religious nature to the subordinate.

At this point in the class instruction, I could sense frustration at the complexity of dealing with religious accommodation. I reminded them that diversity was present throughout culture, including military culture. Even though we wear the same uniform, each Airman has different backgrounds, political affiliations, and philosophical viewpoints. We even have a variety of loyalties to professional sports teams. When I mentioned I was a Dallas Cowboy fan, some would give a cheer. Others would give a moan or jeer. I even heard jokes like, "Chaplain, it is great that the Cowboys have won 5 Super Bowls—too bad we no longer have the technology to watch them!" Or, "The Cowboys are the only team that put their rating on their helmet (one star, implying they are one star in a five-star rating.) Of course, I emphasized that good-natured ribbing of a sports team is fine, but not when it comes to religion.

In dealing with individuals, respect is paramount. Know that though we wear the same uniform, we do not have total uniformity. We come to work as individuals, united on a common mission. I would encourage the class to think about their neighborhood where they lived. Imagine living in a neighborhood where in one house is a family who is Catholic, one is Baptist, one is Muslim, one is Hindu, one is Atheist, etc...Imagine driving home and seeing several cars outside one of the homes, and you discover a death has occurred to a member of one of these families. The most loving, neighboring thing we can do is express our condolences. We ask, "what can I do for you?", if you are in the south, you bring a casserole or a Bundt cake! Your neighborhood mission is to express your sympathy to a grieving family no matter their background, religious affiliation, political leanings, or even their favorite sports team!

In the same, way, as we work alongside a diversity of people and as we meet the mission at hand, we respect others. Personally,

I have found that as a believer, my witness is much stronger, and people are much more receptive to my faith when they are treated with love and respect. In my neighborhood, respect is appreciated, in the workplace, it is the expected standard.

I also emphasized this just wasn't just the opinion or perspective of the chaplain, rather it was codified in Department of Defense Directives and Air Force Instructions.[4] These documents affirm that the free exercise of religion is a basic principle of our nation. They make it policy for commanders to approve accommodation of religious practices when accommodation will not have an adverse effect on military readiness, unit cohesion, standards or discipline. Chaplains are here to help commanders understand the issues in our complex, religiously diverse Air Force community and help Airmen as they seek to practice their faith while serving in the military.

The section on Religious Accommodation during the commander's briefing was always lively. Hopefully, participants were challenged and encouraged. Religious Accommodation can be tricky. They were reminded that when in doubt, ask the chaplain. The chaplain, JAG (legal), and Public Affairs officer are commander resources. Commanders were also encouraged to start with a "yes" to the request and only say "no" when the adverse impact is apparent.

One "Deal or No Deal" question addressed the role of the chaplain and confidentiality. Chaplains are required to hold counseling information as confidential with no exceptions. This requirement is different from the chaplain's civilian counterparts and even military mental health providers.

Question: "A chaplain will hold conversations in confidence, with some exceptions."

Even those these men and women had been in the military for a significant amount of time, the overwhelming majority of the participants would vote thumbs up, Deal—meaning there are exceptions to chaplain confidentiality.

Answer: Many were surprised to hear me say, "No Deal."

Explanation: Military chaplains have no exceptions to confidentiality, even if it is harm to self or harm to others. Several, "what if" questions followed, always with the same response—no exceptions. The inevitable question of "why" was asked. It was then that I could explain that members could be under a pressure cooker of stress. The chaplain was the one person on base that could be trusted to hold the information unconditionally. The opportunity to speak to a chaplain with no fear of reprisal served as a "release" in the pressure cooker to help prevent an explosion. Most members coming to a chaplain are looking for answers and are open to exploring other avenues for help. Though we could refer members to mental health or other helping agencies, the decision must be their own.

I also noted that chaplain confidentiality was military law. Rule 503 of the Military Rules of Evidence states that communications made as a "formal act of religion or as a matter of conscience" to either a chaplain or a chaplain assistant while serving in the capacity of spiritual advisor are considered confidential and are not to be shared with third parties. This confidentiality also applies to inquiries from the command; chaplains cannot be compelled by the command to share information about service members or others seeking their services.[6]

The participants were also reminded that the Chaplain Corps program is the commander's program. The commander, advised by the senior chaplain and chaplain assistant determine the appropriate mix of chapel-based and squadron-based ministries to ensure the Chaplain Corps serves Airmen and their families where they live, work, pray, heal, and grow.[7] Chapels, worksites, flight lines, dormitories, dining facilities, recreational centers, and medical facilities can all become sacred spaces for providing meaningful ministry.[8]

I thoroughly enjoyed these hour-long briefings and loved the give-and-take nature of the conversations that, I hope, led to a greater understanding.

HAVE A BLESSED DAY!

Another word on Religious Accommodation.

On a typical day at Robins AFB, like most bases, cars would be lined up at one of the four gates to gain access. This was a controlled access. All, whether civilian or military, were required to give proper identification. Daily, I would drive to the gate and be greeted by an Airman from Security Forces. I would, if still dark, turn off my headlights, roll down my window, and present him/her my military identification card. He/she would look at it, scan it, and return it back to me. The guard would then, because of my rank, give a smart salute. As I returned the salute, a common phrase I heard from the Airman was, "Welcome to Team Robins, have a blessed day!" I then drove on. What a great way to start the day!

But those innocent and encouraging words, "have a blessed

day" were not pleasing to all. In fact, one person complained. This person did not complain directly to the guard or base leadership. Rather this person complained to a national organization that sees themselves as some sort of "watchdog" of religious freedom. Though the phrase, "have a blessed day" seemed innocent enough—I mean, really, who doesn't want their day to be a blessed or a blessing to others? At least one person, however, saw the words as pushing some religious mandate upon them. The leader of the national organization contacted the Security Forces office directly, conveyed the concern and lodged a complaint. The officer in charge immediately gave an order to the gate guards to cease using the now controversial phrase, "have a blessed day!"

The phrase was eliminated from the greeting. Word spread about the decision throughout the base. It then spread to the media and gained local and national attention. Other military leaders from the higher headquarters got involved and an investigation ensued. Later, that same day, the decision was reversed.

A statement was released by the base:

"We are a professional organization defended by a professional force. Our defenders portray a professional image that represents a base all of Middle Georgia can be proud of. Defenders have been asked to use the standard phrase 'Welcome to Team Robins' in their greeting and can add various follow-on greetings as long as they remain courteous and professional. The Air Force takes any expressed concern over religious freedom very seriously. Upon further review and consultation, the Air Force determined use of the phrase 'have a blessed day' as a greeting is consistent with Air Force standards and is not in violation of Air Force Instructions." [9]

During the Commander's Briefing, I would refer to this event. To many, it seemed so trivial. It took time and resources to deal with a matter that, to many, was insignificant. It did illustrate, however, the volatile nature of religious expression, real or perceived, in our American pluralistic environment. One of the lessons learned was not to react too hastily to a complaint. Gather Subject Matter Experts (SMEs), like the chaplain, JAG, and Public Affairs officer to determine a response. I was reminded of the saying at Al Udeid, "tactical decisions have strategic effects." Commanders were also reminded that "fixing a problem," may lead to other problems. Yes, fixing the problem of one greasy wheel may cause an even greater squeal.

THE BATHSHEBA SYNDROME

Commanders, and leaders at all levels are vulnerable to moral and ethical failure. Throughout my adult life, I have been surprised to hear of leaders who were at the peak of their career, flying high, and then experienced an unexpected crash. I have seen this with political leaders, community leaders, military leaders, and yes, religious leaders. Some stories were played out in the news, some were those I knew personally. Let's be honest, there are some men (usually men) that when the news broke of their infidelity or indiscretion, there was not a lot of surprise.

Many more caused a response like, "Really? Come on, there is no way!" What leads successful men, many times at the height of power and influence to make such reckless decisions?

In 1993, Dean Ludwig and Clinton Longnecker co-authored an article for *The Journal of Business Ethics* titled "The Bathsheba

Syndrome: The Ethical Failure of Successful Leaders." During the mid-2000s, Clinton Longenecker, a University of Toledo, OH professor, became a speaker at various military events describing leaders, high performers who inexplicably experience a moral or ethical meltdown. When military leaders investigated the reason for the administrative removal of an officer (the military jargon is "Detachment for Cause",) or worse, they determined that vast majority had been caught up actions identified in the "Bathsheba Syndrome." The Bathsheba Syndrome is defined as follows: "When successful leaders, with track records of hard work, effectiveness and integrity reach a point in their career where they throw it all away by engaging in an act which is wrong, which they know is wrong, which they know would lead to their downfall if discovered and which they mistakenly believe they have the power to conceal."[9]

Though the concept is discussed in a non-religious framework, the background is rooted in the Biblical story of David's encounter with Bathsheba. As recorded in 2 Samuel 11, David was the successful 50-year-old king of Israel. He was a warrior, visionary, poet, musician, strategist and charismatic leader with a history of principled, faith-based behavior. He truly was a king who had it all! 2 Samuel 11 begins with the phrase, when "Kings go to war..." David, the king was back at the palace. While walking on his balcony, he saw a beautiful woman, Bathsheba, the wife of one of his fighting men, Uriah. Bathsheba was below, bathing. He summoned her to the palace and slept with her. He later learned she was pregnant. After an unsuccessful attempt to cover his tracks, he gives orders that Uriah be placed in the front ranks of the fighting, where Uriah is killed. Upon word of his death, David marries Bathsheba. David feels the matter is settled until the prophet Nathan confronts the king and exposes his sin.

The story of David and Bathsheba gives us an insight on how "success" can lead to a spinning vortex of ethical and moral failure. In the story of David and Bathsheba, three qualities of success led to his failure:

1. In his success, David lost his strategic focus. David was not where he was supposed to be and not doing what he was supposed to do.
2. David's success leads to privileged access. His privileged position, high atop the roof of the palace allowed him to see things that were sheltered at lower levels. His privileged perspective was designed to give him a view to lead his people. He misused this privilege.
3. David's success led to control of resources and an inflated belief in personal ability to control outcomes. David chose to do something that he knew was clearly wrong in the firm belief that through his personal power and control over resources, he could cover it up.

Far too many people have traveled down the road of David. Longnecker notes that successful business leaders and military leaders do unethical/illegal/immoral things because of qualities like "arrogance, ego, "rules don't apply to me" mentality and greed. A successful leader may experience the downside of success— lacking accountability, fear of failure, sense of complacency, an unbalanced social life, and increased stress. A guiding statement for all leaders is: Don't let your success outrun your character. Competency is important, but leaders shall never forget to maintain and build character.

The lessons of David's encounter with Bathsheba can be a warning and instruction for us all. Longnecker states, "Any business leader worth their salt needs to lead by example , which is not an easy thing to do these days. All of us need to be reminded on a regular basis that a leader's reputation and lifetime of work can be destroyed in an instant by making unethical or immoral decisions in the workplace. It is imperative to guard your heart from going down the dark paths that confront all of us."[10]

A Bathsheba Syndrome Study Guide is included in Flight Notes #8

Chaplain's note—Though David did suffer through pain and loss because of his moral failure, God still worked through him. Psalm 51 records his lament, sorrow, and repentance. Though the child Bathsheba was carrying died, she bore another son, Solomon. In the lineage of Jesus recorded in Matthew, descendants of Jesus were not only David, but also Solomon and his mother Bathsheba.

Moral and ethical failures are tragic. Careers can be ruined, marriages can be devastated. Results of the action can be far-reaching. Spiritually, relationships can be tainted; however, in the sight of God, no one is disqualified. Even after our worst day, the grace and mercy of our God is readily available!

YELLOW RIBBON

One of the challenges of serving as a Reservist (TR or IMA) is the inaccessibility to utilize military resources on an ongoing basis. Most reservists live far from their assigned base. These men and women experience the same stresses as their Active-Duty counterparts, especially in a deployed setting. Unlike their Active-Duty counterparts who return to a military environment where they can decompress and debrief with fellow Servicemembers, the reservist goes back to the office or plant or field with little or no support. Even those who are providing spiritual, mental, or emotional care don't have the same connectedness to the military environment and cannot fully understand the difficulties the member faced.

Seeing the need, Congress approved the establishment of the Yellow Ribbon Reintegration Program (YRRP) in January 2008.

As described on the YRRP Website, "The Yellow Ribbon Reintegration Program (YRRP) is a Department of Defense-wide effort to promote the well-being of National Guard and Reserve members, their families and communities, by connecting them with resources throughout the deployment cycle. Through Yellow Ribbon events, Service members and loved ones connect with local resources before, during, and after deployments. Reintegration during post-deployment is a critical time for members of the National Guard and Reserve, as they often live far from military installations and other members of their units. Commanders and leaders play a critical role in assuring that Reserve Service members and their families attend Yellow Ribbon events where they can access information on health care, education and training opportunities, financial, and legal benefits. We work with government partners, including the Small Business Administration, and the Departments of Labor and Veterans Affairs, to provide up-to-date and relevant information to the members of the All-Volunteer force and their families."[11]

The events are normally held at hotels throughout the United States. During the weekends, AFRC personnel, from a variety of disciplines are included as well. Chaplains and chaplain assistants are part of this interdisciplinary team. On occasion a senior-ranking chaplain is asked to provide the key-note speech. This speech is given at the beginning of the event to kick things off. I was given two opportunities, one in Myrtle Beach, South Carolina and one is New Orleans, Louisiana. The following is the key-note speech I delivered in New Orleans:

Thank you for the opportunity to stand before you this morning.

Today, I stand before Heroes—Men and women voluntarily stepping forward to answer our nation's call—a direct link in the 69-year history of the U.S. Air Force Reserve.

Military heroes

Family heroes—Husbands, wives, parents, children

I share with you in your story—I have not only had the privilege to serve in uniform as an Air Force chaplain, but also an Air Force dependent. And, as a young boy, I watched my father, a Sergeant assigned to the Strategic Air Command, walk out the door on his way to a yearlong deployment to Vietnam.

It is a moment in time I will never forget.

Today, let's consider the moments we are given.

Think about the T.V. Remote (while holding one in my hand.) It is one of the greatest inventions of all time. Turn the TV up, turn the TV down, change the channel all from the comfort of your recliner.

Wouldn't it be great if the technology allowed us to use this outside of our TV?

If you got bored with something, just change the

channel—some of you would like to have this now!

Turn the volume up or down, even use the mute button!

Consider the rewind button—maybe you have said something insensitive or unkind to your spouse. You could simply rewind and get a retry. Instead of the unkind word, you could say, "I think you're right" or "I love you, honey."

With this real-life remote, you could push the record button—Be in two places at once. Deployed? You can still be at your son or daughter's soccer game.

When things get too fast, you could push the pause button and take a much needed break.

Fortunately, the pause button is something we can actually experience.

This weekend, make this weekend to take a moment, to experience the power of the pause. For some, you are enjoying this much-needed break, for others the pause is driving you crazy! It is hard to be still and focus.

In studies, survivalists stress the importance of a quiet awareness.

Whether you are surviving a plane crash, stuck on a mountain, trapped in the middle of the ocean, going through cancer, or experiencing the loss of a loved one, a difficult relationship, coming off or going to a deployment, there is power in the pause.

You have to look for it.

This weekend, make this weekend to take a moment, to experience the power of the pause.

A few months back, I was at a church service in Georgia, sitting on the front row, about to deliver a sermon. During the service, there was a group of five year olds sitting next to me. They were there for the music in the service. Before I preached, they would go as a group to another room for a "children's sermon." Before they left the sanctuary, a little boy leaned over and whispered to me: "I have a puppy in my armpit!"

With that, he left with the rest of the group. I was somewhat confused and bewildered at this revelation; however, I quickly dismissed it because it was now time to walk to the pulpit to deliver a sermon.

It was the briefest of conversations from an unlikely source—a little boy sitting on the front row of a church service. I still think about his words and how they have framed other conversations since.

This experience became what I call a "Puppy in My Armpit" (PIMA) moment—a PIMA—a moment when you are on your way to something significant, and your mind becomes redirected, if only for a second.

PIMA moments. PIMA moments are unscripted and unpredictable.

PIMA moments can break up boredom.

As you can imagine, I go to a lot of briefings. Something I have realized in my military life is that briefings are rarely brief.

To help myself stay sharp, one of my hobbies is picking up new phrases at these meetings. These are sayings I rarely hear, sayings that cause me to ponder. Phrases like:

"There is a question mark over the canopy

Lets not act like a dog at a whistler's convention

Cleared Hot, Throttle Back, Spook the Herd

Normative power of the actual

Deep Dive

Don't drown when you deep dive

I need to phone a friend

Who is the closest alligator to the canoe?

We will need to deal with the fur ball

Get the pig through the python"

PIMA moments are found in unlikely places, like hospitals. Years ago, one of my church members, Emmitt was in the ICU. He was dying of cancer. Family and friends gathered and went one by one into the room, but Emmitt was unresponsive. One man, named Tom was a good fishing buddy of the dying man. He was also the local funeral home director. He went in, and came out smiling, He said to the group, "I spoke to Emmitt and his eyes instantly opened."

When I heard these words, I outwardly kept my pastoral demeaner during this very serious time; however, inwardly I was thinking, "If I heard you talking I would have livened up as well!"

A PIMA moment

I have seen PIMA moments at funeral homes, deployments, tense conversations, briefings, and committee meetings. I have seen two married couples in counseling where they are seemingly at each other's throats. But then, something funny is said, a memory is shared and smiles, sometimes laughter breaks out. These moments can change the entire mood of the conversation. I have even seen PIMA moments during Air Force Fitness tests—like the runner who yelled behind me, "I'm not a runner; I was made for football!"

Take a look around, keep a listening ear—PIMA moments are spontaneous, unrehearsed, gentle ways to make it through the day, through the dark valleys, come out with a smile and maybe even some laughter.

These moments of laughter can promote health— Numerous medical studies agree. Doctors tend to agree, "Show me a patient who is able to laugh and play, who enjoys living, and I'll show you someone who is going to live longer." Laughter makes the unbearable bearable and a patient with a well-developed sense of humor has a better chance of recovery than a stoic individual who seldom laughs." True for physical health, true for mental and emotional health.

Push pause, enjoy the occasional puppy in my armpit moments. PIMA moments, pushing the pause button, can be revealing.

A reminder that an insignificant statement, action, expression can be full of a powder keg of emotion or grief.

Important for all of us to be sensitized to what may churning.

Back to the little boy sitting on the front row. I don't really know what was behind the "Puppy in my armpit" statement. I don't think he had a real puppy under his arm, but he may have had a birthmark, or something in there that he was concerned about. I will never know.

Later, using my investigative skills, I Googled, "I've Got a Puppy in my Armpit."

Two articles emerged. One said, "dogs are disgusting and like to smell feet and armpits."

The second article was a bit more intriguing…and enlightening. It noted a connection between a dog sniffing an armpit and the detection of cancer. It told a story of a man who had a cancer under his arm. His dog could sense it and was always wanting to lick under there. Every time he would lay down, the dog would immediately go to that area. After the detection of the cancer and following surgery, the licking stopped.

Maybe there is more to a PIMA moment. Perhaps we should take time to pause and really listen. Maybe we are being told more than we are aware.

If we listen, we may hear someone telling us something that is subtle or indirect, but is secretly eating away at them, like an undetected cancer. Occasionally, they move their pain from a place of silence causing seemingly flippant words to fly out of their mouths. Is anyone really listening, does anyone really care?

Ask most people how they are doing, and they will say, fine! People are telling us that everything is fine, or they are saying nothing at all. Are we really listening? Are we listening to warning signs in our own bodies? Are we listening to those around us that are truly trying to tell us something?

I learned this early in my marriage. We were driving through the country, and my wife Susie would see a roadside peach stand. She would say, "Look there's a peach stand!" I would nod. A little later, she would see another peach stand. She would say, "Look, there's a peach stand!"

I would say something like, "There are a bunch of them out here!"

This would go on and on until finally, she blurted, "Why don't you ever stop?"

Totally confused, I asked, "Stop where?"

With wide eyes and a red face, she said, "At the peach stand!"

I innocently replied, "Well, all you had to do was ask!"

In her own way, she was asking, I just wasn't listening.

During this week, we will hear a lot about resilience. Look around, you are in a city known for its resilience—New Orleans.

During its 200-year history, the New Orleans area has been ravaged repeatedly by hurricanes with the first major hurricane in 1722 destroying nearly every structure in the four-year-old village, including its only church, parsonage and hospital.

These citizens have literally weathered the storm—Hurricane Betsy in 1965, Hurricane Camille in 1969, Hurricane Andrew in 1992, Hurricane Rita in 2005, Hurricanes Gustav and Ike in 2008, and the devastating, Hurricane Katrina in 2005, causing untold financial damage and killing 1465 throughout Louisiana.

Last summer, in Louisiana, the state experienced a catastrophic flood, the worst natural disaster to strike the United States since Hurricane Sandy. And yet, the region moves forward, rebuilding.

In your lives, some have experienced and weathered personal hurricanes that have caused devastation. Those of you who are preparing for a deployment, you carry that history with you. For those of you coming back from deployment, you experienced several things, several moments that stick in your mind—work related, family issues back home, concern for your health and well-being, perhaps some PIMA moments that made you pause and wonder.

Some of the PIMA moments were humorous, some distracting, and some devastating. If these moments were and are increasingly difficult, I encourage you to talk. Talk with family, talk with friends, and talk with counselors and chaplains here. Take advantage of resources that are designed for you. Maybe help out others along the way. This weekend, we are here for you. Take your time to enjoy yourselves and learn a little along the way.

Thank you for the opportunity to speak this morning, prayers are with you in the days ahead.

OTHER SAYINGS HEARD AROUND THE CONFERENCE TABLE

As mentioned in my Yellow Ribbon talk, I had the opportunity to hear and ponder upon many sayings I heard in senior leader Command staff meetings. Some are head scratchers; some are a bit profound. Most of these statements are not those you would hear outside of military circles:

- We have become so process-oriented that we lose the heart factor.
- The ability to learn and adapt faster than the enemy is the only sustainable advantage in modern warfare.
- We need to be strategically predictable and operationally unpredictable.

- Stories are data with a soul.
- Analysis of a valid requirement.
- Tie requirement to the task.
- Responsibility to meet wartime requirement.
- Strategic Imperative Initiatives.
- Normalization of the actual.
- Requirements-based advocacy.
- You need to collect the dots before you connect the dots.
- We have become much more focused on the task than developing the individual.
- We need a fiscally-balanced approach in a resource-constrained environment.
- We don't just recruit Airmen, we retain families.
- Happy Airmen are productive Airmen.
- You may be playing violin, but you are still part of the orchestra. Play in harmony.
- Diversity is being invited to the dance; inclusion is being invited to dance.
- The first job of a leader is to admit reality.
- The nation expects us to go to war in accordance to our values.
- Trust can be lost in a moment.
- Think outside the container.
- We don't want to make a peanut butter spread.
- There is an absence of available appropriations.
- Executable but not funded.
- Low-hanging fruit.
- Let me double tap that.
- Pull up the chocks.
- Everything you say needs to be true, but everything true doesn't need to be said.
- It's hard to sell tickets on a sinking ship.
- If we own the iron, we own the inspection.
- It's not enough to do your best, you've got to know what to

do, then do your best.
- Determining the root-cause analysis.
- We need a strategic pause.
- Who is the closest alligator to the canoe?
- Caught in a frag pattern.
- Framing an understanding of the why.
- Avoid castle-building and castle-defense.
- Move to the sound of the guns.
- See the genius in others.
- Just because it is legal doesn't mean it is advisable.
- I want to help you stay out of the local news.
- Provide the right bandwidth for the task.
- Leverage resources.
- Handle the matter and don't let the matter handle us.
- We need to sing out of the same hymnbook.
- We need a synchronization of processes and situational awareness.
- Not palatable but acceptable.
- Nothing is done in isolation.
- That is outside of our swim lane.
- I see a Delta.
- We have the opportunity to shape the battlespace.
- Credibility is the currency we work with.
- There is a lot of Brocom going on.
- Take away the burrs in the saddle.
- Common sense is not as common as you think.
- Ideas are shared at the speed of trust.
- This is no longer a sustainable platform.
- There is no issue with those currently inside the wire.
- He is driving ahead of his headlights.
- We are coming to a decision point.
- We have reached the 80 percent solution.
- We need more granularity.
- What is the big pole in the tent?

- Once you get in your comfort zone, you begin to degrade your abilities.
- A perfect world seems clear, but we may need a reverse engineering.
- Interoperability in a unity of effort.
- Stay alert, stay alive.
- Email sent is not action taken.
- Major muscle movement.
- I don't want you to look into it, I want you to do it.
- Human Weapons System.
- The way of the past is not meeting the needs of the future.
- Widen the aperture of traditional analysis.
- Credibility is the currency we work with.
- The enemy is always trying to solve our "x."
- Skate where the puck is going to be, not where the puck is.
- We need a seat at the table.
- Architecture does not define mission.
- Use that as a datapoint.
- Stay above the Mendoza line.
- We need to waterfall that to the wings.

And chaplain sayings I have used:

- The Chaplain Corps is also a part of a larger team of helping agencies to provide care for our Airmen.
- Chaplains don't pull a trigger, push a button, or turn a wrench, but we support those who do.
- Our Battle Rhythm.
- Operationally, the Chaplain Corps has a direct line to the spiritual pillar of Comprehensive Airman Fitness.
- Yes, chaplains are found at the bottom of the cliff tending to those who have crashed. We are also at the top of the cliff with warning signs.
- Take time to focus on the heart and soul of the warrior.

- MBWA—"Ministry by walking around."
- Tune our ears to truly listen.
- There is music in a rest
- HAF (Chief of Chaplains office) determines the "what." AFRC determines the "how."
- Thinking pastorally goes beyond comfort.
- HDLD (High Demand, Low Density) chaplains are needed.
- We need faces for the spaces.
- We spend so much time on the work of the Lord and not enough time for the Lord of the work.
- We need to keep the Faith-Based Common Operating Picture in mind.
- We are taking a passive position on this.
- Never devalue the sacrifice of those participating in a noble endeavor.
- When a river encounters a rock, it either flows over or around. Eventually, the water makes the rock smooth. Your choice—when facing obstacles, you can either fight, flee, or flow.
- Standing by to assist if required.
- When you can't trace His hand, you have to trust His heart.
- Be aware of the Airman Ministry Planning process: Focus, Leverage, Execution, and Accountability.
- (And the mouthful) We need to leverage data to demonstrate the role that spirituality and religion can play in improving health in every domain of Comprehensive Airman Fitness.

BEGINNING OF TRANSITION

In the summer of 2019, I was on a military Temporary Tour of Duty (TDY) in San Antonio, TX. While there, I received a phone call from a friend from college who was a pastor of a church outside of Marble Falls, Texas. He said that a church near Whitney, Texas was seeking a pastor. He asked if I was interested. The call caught me a bit off guard. My desire, after retirement, was to get back to Texas. But the conversation to move seemed premature. My immediate response was, "Thanks for thinking about me, but the timing is off." My orders were scheduled to go through November 2020. I still had 18 months on my military commitment. I told him, "Let's talk more in a few months." Before hanging up, he sent me the website address of the church. I took a look, and then another.

Though the timing was off, the opportunity intrigued me. I was not able to release it out of my mind. Finally, I called my friend and said, "Feel free to send the resume to this church and we will just see what happens." Long story short, the pastor search committee was interested in me, to the point I took some days of leave and traveled to Texas. In February 2020, Susie and I came to the White Bluff Chapel, an interdenominational church near Whitney, Texas, in view of a call—meaning I would preach and the congregation would decide if I was the right choice. The call to become their pastor was a unanimous "yes." In anticipation of this possibility, I had shortened my orders to August 2020. The church was willing to wait six months in order for me to fulfill my military obligation. This was the new path set before me, but the path was about to take a hard curve.

COVID-19

Shortly after this February decision, a worldwide epidemic was spreading across the world. In March, states began to implement shutdowns in order to prevent the spread of COVID-19. The wearing of masks, social distancing, travel advisories, and vaccines became the norm.

When I was at SOUTHCOM, one of the scenarios we exercised was a pandemic. At the time, I thought it was a waste of time. With modern medicine, how realistic was a world-wide pandemic, something we hadn't experienced since 1918? .

But plans were in place. The Department of Defense provided support and care where needed. In April, in New York City, the USNS Comfort treated 64 patients. 366 military medical personnel, many reservists, were augmenting New York City hospitals. As the virus swept across the nation a major disaster declaration had been issued in all 50 states for the first time in American history. By the end of April, the United States surpassed 1 million confirmed coronavirus cases, a third of all cases around the globe. At this point, over 56,000 had died. By May, U.S. COVID-19 related deaths surpassed 100,000. By July, the death toll surpasses 150,000 and the number kept growing.

For the military, it was important not to lose focus on other emerging threats. In the midst of the pandemic, we had to maintain vigilance and a business-as-usual approach. Like much of America, the workplace was severely affected. Social distancing was in effect which limited the number of individuals in each office. With minimum manning in effect, we learned the value of technology and working remotely. Coming to work was somewhat eerie. For years, I had become accustomed to the hustle and bustle of work in our building and offices. Now it was a ghost-town. The parking lot that was normally full was now sparse. Any social interaction involved masks and social distancing. The virus caused a cloud of uncertainty and doubt to be cast over us all.

On a personal side, incredibly, in the heart of the pandemic we bought a home in the community of White Bluff in Whitney, sold our home in Perry, and coordinated the move of our house furnishings to Texas. The sale of the house in Perry happened much sooner than we expected. I mean, really, who buys a house in the middle of a pandemic? Susie and I were looking to live in temporary housing for the next three months. Out of safety concerns (increase exposure to COVID-19) and practical reasons, I requested leadership to allow me to move to Texas and continue my work via teleconference and other media tools. Since at this point, the majority of the Command was working from home, leadership agreed as long as I was able to come back to Robins if needed. I enthusiastically agreed and spent three months telecommuting from my home in Texas.

Retirement Ceremony

In mid-August, I returned to Robins in order to complete my out processing and participate in a somewhat creative retirement ceremony. It is customary to have a ceremony at a large auditorium, or in the case of a chaplain, at the base chapel. The event would include family members, friends, and coworkers at AFRC. As a chaplain, I provided many invocations at these type of celebratory events. In our COVID world, large gatherings were no longer possible. So, our Public Affairs officer agreed to allow the use of the base studio for the ceremony. It was recorded with the ability to distribute to those interested. The participants in the studio ceremony included myself, Maj General Flournoy, Chaplain Danford, and a handful of media personnel manning the cameras and producing the event.

During the ceremony, Gen Flournoy said some kind words and

recalled some highlights of my career. Then, it was time for the retirement order to be read. With myself and Gen Flournoy standing at attention, Ch Danford read the following:

"Attention to orders: Department of the Air Force, Washington, District of Columbia, by order of the Secretary of the Air Force, special order number EL2863, Colonel Randy A. Marshall, Robins AFB, Georgia, you are relieved from military duty, with Headquarters Air Force Reserve Command, Chaplain, retired effective 17 August 2020 in the grade of Colonel by the Secretary of the Air Force."

As the recent retiree, I shared the following:

"Thank you, General Flournoy, for your kind and gracious words. I appreciate Chaplain Danford for the reading of the retirement order and Ch Matuska for setting all of this up.

Last week, General Flournoy asked me what I would miss the most in retirement. I know it sounds a bit cliché, but I will definitely miss the people. I have been honored to serve under great leadership including Gen Flournoy and Gen Scobee. The AFRC Chaplain Corps team has been remarkable as we have sought to carry out the vision of providing spiritual care and advisement to those answering our nation's call.

I appreciate each of you and your dedication to the work and the ability, now and then. to have a little fun.

I am grateful for the undergirding of church support, many who are watching today. It was a great privilege to serve as your pastor and most recently, interim pastor. I am grateful for the loving support of my family, as Gen Flournoy mentioned; my sister, Sandy and her husband, Bob; my daughter Amanda and grandchild Matthew; my son, Blake, and his wife Lindsey (and later children

Emery and Bennett), and other extended family.

Certainly, I am grateful for my wife, Susie. I am thankful that every time I began the sentence with, "Honey, what do you think about...," she didn't just run! Whether it was a new move or a new adventure, her attitude was always, "let's go!" So our Air Force adventure is behind us, a new adventure is before us.

I am holding to the words and the promises of a military leader long ago who said,

"Be strong and courageous, for the Lord your God is with you wherever you go."

So, friends and family, thank you for joining us today. This chapter has closed. Another begins. And the adventure continues.

Let's pray together, Our Father, we thank you Lord for the opportunity to look at days past. Father, we thank you that we have been able to influence others, and certainly a host of individuals have influenced us. Guide us as we continue on this day and the days ahead as we seek to know and follow Your perfect will. We pray these things in Jesus' name, Amen.

Thank you again for being a part of this ceremony. God's blessing upon each of you as your own adventure continues!"

On the video produced, the following closing words scrolled:

"AFRC wishes Chaplain Randy Marshall and his family a future filled with blessings, peace, and happiness.

People say one person can't make a difference in the world, but we know that isn't true, because we've seen the difference you make in the lives of those around you.

Faith is making yesterday a steppingstone, today a new beginning, tomorrow a limitless possibility.

Thank you for 30 years and 8 months of outstanding and exemplary service.

May your paths be filled with simple joys and blessing without end."

With that, this chapter of my life has concluded, The Marshall Chronicles: Aim High Edition is closed, but a new adventure awaits and a new story unfolds in this trilogy, The Marshall Chronicles: White Bluff Edition.

Epilogue

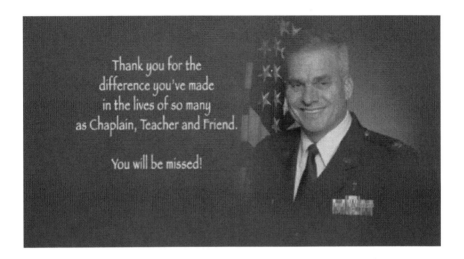

Thank you for the difference you've made in the lives of so many as Chaplain, Teacher and Friend.

You will be missed!

In the AFRC Command Chaplain's office there was a framed picture of myself, the Command Chaplain. I mentioned several times that though it was an honor to have my picture on the wall, there would come a day when the picture would be replaced. When replaced, there would be no fanfare, someone would simply slide my picture out and put the picture of my successor in. We should never think that we are irreplaceable. We are valued and hopefully remembered, but in our offices at least, we are replaceable. Hopefully, we have provided training, instruction, and influence to those who continue to carry on the work.

Within the Chaplain's office, and throughout AFRC, some remained, some moved on, some moved up, and some retired. New staffs were formed.

New challenges and opportunities were faced. As I was

walking out the door, a brand-new Service was taking shape, the Space Force. The Air Force Chaplain Corps including AFRC would be providing Chaplain support to provide spiritual support and religious advisement to the Space Force Guardians. The Chaplain Candidate program was undergoing some changes that would enhance recruiting efforts. Full-time Chaplain Corps support at select AFRC locations was becoming reality. New ministries and opportunities continued to materialize.

I am grateful and humbled that by God's grace, I was able to be part of the incredible adventure of being a United States Air Force chaplain. 30 years and 8 months flew by. I was involved in this endeavor in a much greater way than I could have ever imagined. My part-time service helped shape me as a minister. The full-time service was an unexpected blessing that provided an even greater depth of understanding and ministry opportunities. Coming out of Seminary, if you had told me the military path I was going to travel, I probably would have told you it was highly unlikely, or even impossible. But we know….

It always seems impossible until it's done…
and with God, all things are possible!

Flight Notes

Flight Notes #1

HOME IMPROVEMENT STUDY GUIDE

Building Materials—Commit or Submit?

Ephesians 5:22-33, 1 Peter 3:1-9
1. According to these passages, what is the role of the husband in marriage?
2. What is the role of the wife?
3. What does Paul mean when he writes that marriage is a "profound mystery?
4. What does Peter mean when he writes that the wife is a "weaker vessel?"

Building Materials—Commitment

Genesis 2:18-25
1. Why was Eve created?

2. At this point in the Biblical story, Adam and Eve were living in the perfection of the Garden of Eden. How was their relationship different than couples today?

3. What is the significance of Genesis 2:25?

THE FOUNDATION

Read Matthew 7:24-27

1. In this passage, what does the rock represent?

2. Why is building upon the rock so important?

3. What kind of storms can a marriage face?

4. In what ways can a home fall?

NEGOTIATION

Read Job 4:8, Galatians 6:7 and James 3:18

1. How does the farming principle of sowing and reaping relate to family relationships?

Read Galatians 5:22

2. What fruit is most evident in your marriage?

Least evident?

THE PLANS

Read Proverbs 24:3-4

1. Where is the source of wisdom?

2. What keeps us from relying on the wisdom of God?

3. Christian speakers say we should "attach ourselves to God". How can we do that as couples?

4. What do you think are some "rare and beautiful treasures" that

you want in your home?

Flight Notes #2

TEAM RANDOLPH MARRIAGE POST-DEPLOYMENT MARRIAGE RETREAT

Teaching Outline:
Friday
Introduction:
re·treat (rĭ-trēt')
1: (military) withdrawal of troops to a more favorable position to escape the enemy's superior forces or after a defeat
2: a place of privacy; a place affording peace and quiet
3: (military) a signal to begin a withdrawal from a dangerous position
4: (military) a bugle call signaling the lowering of the flag at sunset
5: an area where you can be alone [syn: hideaway]
6: withdrawal for prayer and study and meditation; "a religious retreat"
Isaiah 40
> "Those who wait upon the Lord will mount up with wings like eagles, they will run and not be weary, they will walk and not faint."

As a minister, I love to see people soar. Fly. Interesting thing about the flight of an eagle—soar on the air below, on desert thermals. Isaiah reminds us that we don't always soar, sometimes we run, sometimes we walk, sometimes we experience life at a crawl.

We experience them all.

But the journey is all what I call the Great Adventure—

sometimes flying high without a care in the world, sometimes feet cut and hands bloody, ready to give up.

Challenge—press on, press forward.

Session 1: The Journey

We are all on a journey. From the time that we are born to the time that we die, we are all moving in a certain direction.

There are three different kinds of travelers...

First, there are the ___hermits.___ They move in from the outside, settle in caves and stay in one place until they die.

Second, there are the ___nomads.___ They have a lot of movement, they are always on the go; however, their movement is always circular, never moving to a particular destination.

Third, there are the ___pilgrims.___ They have both movement and direction, meaning and purpose.

At the end of our life's journey, and a headstone is place on our grave, there will be a dash between the date that we were born and the date that we die. How we live in that dash will define the kind of travel plans in which we have chosen.

Peter Marshall, in one of his famous prayers before the U.S. Senate prayed:

Forbid it, Lord that our roots become too firmly attached to this earth, that we should fall in love with things. Help us to understand that the pilgrimage of this life is but an introduction, a preface, a training school for what is to come...

As a couple, you do not travel this journey alone. This weekend, you will be encouraged to consider your journey together, taking a look at the past, present, and future.

It has been said that there are three stages of marriage. The ___romance___ stage is characterized by the newness of the relationship.

The ___reality___ stage is pictured when the newness

wears off and one becomes more aware of the spouse's faults and weaknesses.

Illustration: One young man—married for a couple of weeks. Dear, would you mind if I pointed out a few faults that I've noticed about you. She replied, Certainly, just remember that it was those faults that kept me from getting a better man than you!

The final stage is the _____resignation_____ or _____reconstruction_____ stage. This is a continual process that requires the couple to decide their direction together, resign or reconstruct.

Many spend a lot of time focusing on the duties of life: completing suspenses (deadlines), meeting job requirements, carpooling the kids, attending games, cooking meals, mowing lawns, etc…that we lose sight of the meaning behind it all. We get so busy doing life that we fail to live life.

This weekend is a crossroad on your journey. You can make it a weekend where you just get away, or a weekend where you experience a fresh start, a new beginning. Marriage can be a drudgery to be endured or an adventure to be enjoyed.

Consider intimacy, passion, and commitment

Today, how would you rate the emotional and physical levels of your relationship?

What about your level of commitment?

Discussion: Passion and intimacy fluctuate, but commitment should never waver.

Our physical and emotional levels will continually fluctuate; however, our commitment level should always be the same.

Commitment is the glue that holds the marriage together.

SATURDAY

Session 2: Pitfalls on the Journey

The marriage journey is an adventure. It is full of ups and downs, highs and lows. Sometimes the road is smooth and wide, other times it is bumpy and narrow. The wise traveler is one that anticipates trouble and is able to negotiate around it. These troubles could be labeled "pitfalls."

A pitfall is something or someone that interrupts our forward progress. Some pitfalls are small and merely make the ride temporarily uncomfortable. Others are so wide and deep that escape seems impossible, and the situation appears impassable.

Group discussion questions:

1. What are some of the pitfalls in marriage, particularly military marriages?

2. What are some solutions to get out of the pit or to avoid the pit in the future?

The ancient Hebrews saw the pit as a literal or figurative reference to the grave. The abyss was so deep that the one stuck on the bottom felt like the living dead.

Sometimes the pit is so deep that we need some outside help. In the Bible, the Psalmist writes:

I waited patiently for the Lord;

He turned to me and heard my cry.
He lifted me out of the slimy pit,
out of the mud and mire;
He set my feet on a rock
and gave me a firm place to stand.
He put a new song in my mouth,
a hymn of praise to our God.
Many will see and fear
and put their trust in the Lord.
Psalm 40:1-3

No one can make you stay in the pit. Also, no one can make you leave, not even God, it is a choice that only you can make.

Whether you are spiritually minded or not, seek the help of those outside of your relationship to gain a better perspective and a bigger picture of your marital journey.

Pitfalls on the journey, both large and small, are inevitable. Are you willing to face them together? Are you willing to seek help beyond yourself?

Session 3: Accident (or otherwise) Forgiveness

A national insurance company advertises that they offer "accident forgiveness." Insurance premiums don't automatically increase when an accident occurs. How open are you to giving and receiving forgiveness?

SATURDAY AFTERNOON GUIDELINES

1. Relax
2. Eat
3. Enjoy the Riverwalk. Resist the temptation to go home and "take care of things."
4. Avoid checking your e-mail, voice-mail, etc…
5. Focus on your relationship
    - Avoid talking about the kids, bills, work, etc…
    - Formulate some tangible ways to strengthen and rekindle your relationship. Be honest, be open, be kind.
    - Write these things down and bring them back to Sunday morning session. Because of the personal nature of these thoughts, you will not be asked to share them with the rest of the group.
6. Bonus assignment (for those willing to go the extra mile)
    - Approach five couples that you do not know—particularly those with some

"maturity"—who appear to be in love. Say something like, "We're here this weekend on a marriage retreat. Our speaker asked us to find some couples that seem to be genuinely in love, what's your secret?"

- Write their responses and bring back to Sunday morning session.

SUNDAY

Session 4: Charting a Course for the Future

Later this morning, you will turn in your hotel room key, pack your clothes, and return home—the retreat will be over, but the journey will continue. When you go back home, you are faced with another crossroad. Will I leave what I've learned back at the riverwalk, or will I use this weekend experience for a time of renewal? Will my marriage be a drudgery to be endured or an adventure to be enjoyed?

Take time to chart a course for the future before the turbulence of life hits.

For those who took the challenge of yesterday's question #6, what responses did you receive?

Small group time for couples:

Chart your course for the future. Think in terms of goals and action steps. What are three goals that we would like to strive for in the coming days and what actions can I take to accomplish those goals?

Goal 1:

_____

Action steps:

_____

_____

Goal 2:
Action steps:

Goal 3:
Action steps:

Session 5: GPS for the journey

At any given moment, there are 24 operational Global Positioning System satellites orbiting in space, flying some 11,000 miles overhead. The satellites, operated by the U.S. Air Force, orbit every 12 hours. Ground stations are used to precisely track each satellite's orbit. At any given time, there are 6 or 7 that are accessible to a GPS receiver.

The satellites' signals, moving at the speed of light allow the user on earth to determine his/her position.

A GPS receiver programmed for "relationships" would be a great tool for those attempting to navigate the uncertainties of the marital journey. It would be great to know our present location, our desired destination and the best path to take us there.

Though we don't have such a device, we do have three coordinates that can help synchronize and energize us along the

way. These three are <u>Faith, Family,</u>
and <u> Friends.</u>

The journey of marriage can be adventurous, but it can also be treacherous. Circumstances and events beyond our control can make us feel disconnected, disjointed, and disengaged. No matter where you find yourself in the AEF (Deployment) cycle, remember that life still moves forward. Lean on the support of those who can provide perspective and purpose as together you celebrate your marriage—the Great Adventure!

Flight Notes #3

PATRIOT DEFENDER CHAPLAIN LEADERSHIP COURSE

Lesson Plan Subjects and Objectives :

The instructor training at Patriot Defender was an eleven-hour block of instruction. Though this time frame fit into the curriculum requirements at Patriot Defender, the instruction could have been divided into two or more blocks of time. Four Plans of Instructions (POIs) provided a comprehensive view of the unique influence of the USAF chaplain both in the past and the present. While a chaplain's influence is part of the fabric of military history, his or her role, especially in leadership settings, has been scrutinized and analyzed. It was important for the student to recognize the rich history of chaplain involvement as he or she viewed the challenges and the opportunities in a highly diverse and pluralistic world.

Plan of Instruction (POI)1:

The Call to Leadership The objective of this lesson plan was to ensure that each student understood the historical impact of military chaplain involvement and the priority of Air Force chaplain leadership today. The presentation highlighted the unique presence of the American military chaplain since the Revolutionary War. The Air Force Chaplain builds upon this tradition. A major ministry priority is chaplain leadership. The outline of instruction included:

- The Leadership
- Historical Background on Chaplain Involvement
- Air Force Chaplain Corps Vision
- Air Force Chaplain Corps Sphere of Influence

The chaplains were reminded and challenged that personally and professionally, they must uphold the standard in moral, ethical, and spiritual behavior. They must be able to provide a prophetic voice even in the friction and fog of war. In addition, they must be proficient in providing spiritual, ethical, and moral guidance to Airmen of all ranks. They can be a significant —force multiplier by being a source of information and inspiration to today's Air Force community. Because of the increasingly diverse and pluralistic 21st century world, this can be quite a challenge.

Though the Chaplain Corps itself is very diverse, it is imperative that a common vision is embraced. In the instruction, it was noted that the USAF chaplain vision, core processes, and core competencies all address leadership as a primary chaplain role. The chaplain should recognize and embrace this role as a vital part of chaplain ministry in the 21st Century.

POI 2: Leadership to Self

The objective of POI 2 was to ensure that each student had an understanding of personal leadership. Leadership to self provides inner guidance and validates ministry to others. The presentation addressed the inner virtues, theological underpinnings, and personality types that affect outward behavior. Leadership to self should continually be emphasized and exercised. The outline of the instruction included:

- Leadership Virtues
- Theological View of Leadership
- Leadership Personalities

Though there are several desirable leadership virtues, writers on leadership from across diverse spectrums focus on character and integrity. A chaplain's ethical leadership begins with developing one's own character and knowledge of ethics. The success of a chaplain's ministry is dependent upon the chaplain's character. In this sense then, a chaplain is a virtue ethicist, believing that developing a virtuous life will lead to, if not result in, ethical living. Clearly, a chaplain's true character will be known and will determine one's effectiveness in ministry. Building upon a chaplain's faith tradition, one is guided in the qualities of character that typify religious leaders. As a foundational minimum, a chaplain must embody the Air Force core values before even attempting to be an ethical leader or advising leaders on ethics.

Students were also challenged to consider their own theological and philosophical perspectives. Chaplains should possess a broader and deeper worldview than their professional counterparts. A leadership philosophy that is clearly thought-out and articulated can open doors of ministry throughout the chain of command.

POI 3: Leadership to the Institution

The objective POI 3 was to ensure that each student understood the unique opportunities and challenges of ministering in an institutional environment. The presentation addressed the diversity and pluralism that today's Air Force chaplain encounters. Military chaplains in the twenty-first century must embrace crucial roles that define and clarify their presence in an institutional setting. Individual, faith group, and personal goals should be integrated to optimize fulfillment and effectiveness. This presentation was at the heart of the chaplain leadership training curriculum that integrated teaching with real-life application. The outline of the instruction included:
• Tensions Surrounding Chaplain Leadership to the Institution
• Utilizing the Getzels-Guba Model

- Chaplain Corps Crucial Roles
- Advising Command: Ethical, Moral, and Spiritual Leadership

In order to thrive in military chaplain ministry, the minister must recognize the tension of meeting personal, denominational, and institutional needs. These tensions include being —under command, the outward perception of military Chaplaincy, ministry in a pluralistic environment, and one's personal ministry calling. The Getzels-Guba model of social behavior was introduced to explain the dynamics of social behavior in a given institutional environment, relating role expectations and role perceptions of individuals or groups operating within a given institution and cultural social structure. When a person's behavior meets institutional role expectations, he has obviously adjusted‖ to the role. When a person is able to meet all of his personal needs while simultaneously meeting the institution's role expectations, Getzels and Guba say that he is integrated.

The fact that the chaplain belongs to two institutions— military and ecclesiastical, makes this integration process even more challenging. The chaplain can excel in twenty-first century ministry by recognizing his or her unique roles. First, the military chaplaincy provides the best resource for protecting and facilitating the First Amendment right of the free exercise of religion.[1]

This is the bedrock legal and institutional justification for the existence of the military chaplaincy. Second, Chaplains uniquely function within a command in areas of human wholeness. They serve in the military command with a special focus on the individual. Chaplains serve alongside the military member. They are not embedded with the unit as a reporter from the outside, rather, they are incarnate with the unit representing the presence of the Holy from within the institution. Third, the chaplain in combat, as a helpful bystander, is an ideal point of discernment for the potential growth of moral disengagement. A consequence of a chaplain's presence in a unit is his or her ability to enter into the life of those in combat settings. The chaplain can offer a humanizing point of reference to buffer against the moral disengagement by personnel who are drawn into moral vertigo by the emotional and ethical demands of warfare. The chaplain can provide a moral presence that offers preemptive ethical guidance in seeing whether the conditions of combat or insurgency operations are moving members of a unit into unhealthy moral directions. No other member of the unit is so uniquely positioned to provide this guidance to the command.

In this POI, the Just War Tradition was presented as a theological and philosophical framework of understanding. Fourthly, the chaplain can be crucial in helping troops unpack the moral, spiritual, and emotional impact of traumatic experiences. The chaplain, as a spiritually-identified, caring individual can assist the military member in the emotional and spiritual recovery process in both the combat environment and home base reintegration. These four roles were highlighted with an awareness and ability of the chaplain to advise command concerning ethical, moral, and spiritual issues. The chaplain should see himself or herself as a key member of the commander's staff to inform, protect, and provide information concerning spiritual and religious issues. One model that can help in the decision-making process is the OODA loop designed by former Air Force pilot and military strategist, Col. John Boyd. This decision-making model consists of four overlapping and interacting processes: Observe, Orient, Decide and Act. The OODA loop is a simple tool to be used emphasizing a —situational awareness‖ mentality. It can help to not only clarify the moral, ethical, or spiritual issue but also move the person to action or help the person evaluate a decision already made.

POI 4: Leadership to Chapel Teams

The objective of POI 4 was to ensure that each student had an understanding of the formation of working teams and team dynamics. The student should know the value of chapel teams and the synergy that comes from unit cohesiveness. The presentation would address the teamwork that is necessary for chaplain personnel to be fully effective in ministry to the Air Force community. The importance of the leader in the team building and team sustaining process was highlighted. Deployment scenarios were shared and discussed. The outline of the instruction included:

- Curahee——We stand alone, together
- The Leadership Situation
- The Synergy of a Team
- Conflict Management
- Deployment Case Studies

Throughout the two-week training, the students watched the film series entitled, "Band of Brothers." This was used as a training tool to immerse the students into a war-time mentality during this deployment-based training. Issues relating to Post-Traumatic Stress Disorder were discussed as well as aspects of leadership in an environment where teamwork is paramount. The title of the first episode was "Currahee," a Cherokee word meaning "stands alone." It became the cry of the 506th Paratroopers Regiment during World War II. Easy Company, as they were called, adapted the theme to be, "We stand alone, together." Students discussed some of the unique individuals in the series and their motivation to work together. They were also asked, "How does this apply to the Chaplain Corps?" Students were reminded of the teamwork that is necessary to fulfill the mission of the USAF Chaplain Corps. The individuals may function as a working group; however, great ministry occurs when the groups can become a synergistic team. In any team or group, conflicts arise. The chaplain leader needs to be aware of this dynamic. Many chaplains have responded that the most difficult aspect of deployment was working with fellow chaplains or not getting along with their supervisor.

Developing proper conflict management skills and heightened interpersonal relationships can sustain a chaplain team as they stand alone, together. The instructional portion of the training was reinforced by individual deployment scenarios. These scenarios were enacted during the Simulated Training Exercise (STX). While Chaplain Corps students were interacting and participating with Security Forces students during the STX, the instructor interjected a scenario. With the coordination of Security Forces instructors, Security Forces students were participants in this teaching exercise. The intent of the scenario was to place the chaplain in a stressful situation and evaluate his or her reaction. A chaplain instructor observed and gave helpful feedback once the scenario was complete.

Flight Notes #4

Military Chaplains working with Faith-Based Nongovernmental Organizations in Disaster Relief Operations
OPERATION UNIFIED RESPONSE:

    1. Background
          a. The Situation

On 12 Jan 2010, the strongest earthquake in Haiti in more than 200 years, measuring 7.0 on the Richter scale, struck the impoverished Caribbean nation. The earthquake's epicenter was south-west of Haiti's capital, Port-au-Prince, which suffered extensive damage. The nearby cities of Carrefour and Jacmel and other areas to the west and south of Port-au-Prince were also affected, with the town of Léogâne 80% destroyed. Over 220,000 were killed and over 300,000 were injured. Over 3 million people required humanitarian assistance of some kind. The president of Haiti, Rene Garcia Preval declared a national state of emergency and requested assistance from the United States and other members of the international community.

          b. The Response

In response to the government of Haiti's request and U.S.

Ambassador to Haiti, Kenneth H. Merten's declaration of disaster, U.S. government agencies initiated their disaster plans. The United States Agency for International Development Office of U.S. Foreign Disaster Assistance (USAID/OFDA) became the lead federal agency. They immediately implemented an emergency response program and deployed a Disaster Assistance Response Team to Haiti.

The U.S. Southern Command, as a supporting agency in the relief effort, established Joint Task Force-Haiti to oversee U.S. military relief efforts in Haiti and appointed LTG Kenneth Keen, USA, as the joint force commander (JFC). More than 25,000 U.S. military and DOD personnel, 18 U.S. ships, and more than 60 aircraft provided support to the operation. They facilitated relief and care to more than three million Haitians who were affected by the earthquake. The mission was designated "Operation UNIFIED RESPONSE."

c.   The Role of the Chaplain Corps

When Joint Task Force-Haiti (JTF-H) was formed, the USSOUTHCOM Command Chaplain, Ch, Col Jeff Dull immediately deployed CH (COL) Kevin Turner and SFC Jesse Miles, Command Chaplain Religious Support Team (RST) at Special Operations Command South, to serve as the JTF-H Command Chaplain and NCOIC. As the U.S. Navy, Army, Coast Guard, Marines, and Air Force deployed personnel to the Joint Operations Area (JOA), RSTs deployed with these units, providing spiritual care to their military members. Because of the nature of the mission, RSTs were also exposed to various national and international entities that had been mobilized to provide humanitarian relief in the context of a unified action.

Because of the chaplain's military training coupled with his/her religious leader credentials, he/she can be a force multiplier in foreign Humanitarian Assistance/Disaster Relief (HA/DR) operations.

2. Faith-Based Non-Governmental Organizations (NGOs) Contributions
   a. The church or other faith-based organizations, including traditional faith healers, can be viewed as the largest, most stable, and most extensively dispersed nongovernmental organization in any country.

Faith organizations are respected within communities, and most have existing resources, structures, and systems upon which to build. They possess the human, physical, technical, and financial resources needed to support and implement small- and large-scale initiatives. They can undertake these actions in a very cost-effective manner due to their ability to leverage volunteers and other resources with minimal effort. Community-based and faith-based organizations are on the forefront of meeting human needs around the world and are excellent implementing partners because of their dedication to results, their ability to reach the grassroots of society, and their capacity to mobilize societies for positive change.

   b. Faith-based NGOs in humanitarian operations bring responsiveness and long-term commitment.

Faith based organizations respond quickly to difficult situations, accepting challenges other institutions ignore or quickly abandon when they linger or become unfashionable. They take a holistic approach, melding the spiritual, physical, mental and social aspects of health and balance. Religious leaders can influence communities, societies, nation, and the course of human events.[2]

   c. Relationship of the NGOs with the Armed Forces

NGOs do not operate within the military or governmental hierarchy or the chain of command. Therefore, any relationship between the armed forces and an NGO is best characterized as a professional or circumstantial association. Generally, coordination between military forces and NGOs is facilitated through the UN, USAID, or DOS. The military force ordinarily orchestrates this interaction with other agencies and organizations through the activities of a civil-military operations center (CMOC).

NGOs are frequently present and actively engaged in development activities when U.S. forces arrive. They often remain long after military forces have departed. Some NGOs are independent, diverse, flexible, grassroots-focused, primary relief providers. Others, however, provide a channel for funds and collaborate with other primary relief NGOs (usually local) to carry out the programs. Because they can respond quickly and effectively to crises, NGOs can lessen the civil-military resources that commanders would otherwise have to devote to an operation.

The first line of security foremost to NGOs is their adherence to strict principles of impartiality, neutrality, and independence. Actions that blur the distinction between relief workers and military forces may be perceived as a threat to these principles. Military forces seek to establish a climate of cooperation with NGOs. Missions to support NGOs are short term, usually necessitated by extraordinary events. In most situations, the NGOs need logistics, communications, and security capabilities. However, in such missions, the role of the armed forces is to enable, not perform NGO tasks.

Often U.S. military assistance has proven to be the critical difference that enabled success of an operation. Commanders understand that mutually beneficial arrangements between the armed forces and NGOs may determine the success of the military operation. NGOs and military units both have significant incentives to coordinate and collaborate. NGOs need many things from the military: including logistical assistance, communications, intelligence and protection. (FM 3-07 6 October 2008).

3. Chaplain Guidance in working with NGOs
    a. Chaplains may advise the commander and staff members on various religious dynamics within the

operational area. On occasion, chaplains may also be tasked with accomplishing certain liaison functions, particularly with indigenous religious leaders and faith-based NGOs operating in the operational area Joint Publication (JP) 1-05.

b. The United States Government (USG) supports faith-based organizations, but USG policy strictly states that USG assistance must be distributed based on need, not based on religious affiliation or for the purpose of influencing the religious beliefs of a population (JP 3-29).

c. Chaplains may accompany elements of the joint force as they distribute relief supplies or have other interactions (e.g., security patrols) with the local populace (JP 3-29).

d. Chaplains' status as members of the clergy/endorsed religious leaders provides them with credentials no one else will have. It also gives them access to certain leaders, populations, and locations.

e. Humanitarian aid is heavily symbolic—hence political. Interveners generally view the provision of aid as a positive response to a humanitarian crisis; however, the perception of preference of one group over another can exacerbate an existing crisis.

f. Chaplains should be mindful that cultural differences exist in the military-civilian relationship in areas such as decision making, accountability, flexibility, aims and expectations, time perspective, and trust.

g. Chaplains can significantly enhance their effectiveness with NGOs if they are at the appropriate location as the operation unfolds. Participation in CMOCs, Humanitarian Assistance Survey Teams (HASTs), and Joint Task Force (JTF) Assessment Teams to assist in coordination of NGO-military activities is recommended in JTF doctrine and policy.

h. When conducting relief activities, military personnel should wear uniforms or other distinctive clothing that distinguishes them from relief workers.

i. U.S. Armed Forces should not describe relief workers as force multipliers or partners‖ of the military. Their independence and autonomy should be protected.

j. The term "coordinated" can be divisive. Generally, NGOs define the term as talking and sharing information, the military uses it to mean command and control in a given situation.

k. Larger NGOs will often provide a military liaison staff member to manage military interface.

l. NGOs, while auxiliaries in the humanitarian services of their governments and subject to the laws of their respective countries, must always maintain their autonomy so that they can act in accordance with the principles of their organization.

m. Any religious activities of humanitarian organizations must take place in a separate time or place from USG-funded activities. Participation from USG members must be voluntary.

4. Extraordinary challenges in the Haiti humanitarian relief effort

   a. In the days following the earthquake, a massive international relief effort was rapidly put in place in spite of extraordinary logistical challenges, particularly the earthquake's destruction of entry points into Port-au-Prince.

   b. Damage to Port-au-Prince's seaport forced aid agencies to try to supply a city of three million using the sole runway at the capital's airport, plus some overland transport from the Dominican Republic.

   c. The need for a continued international humanitarian response was assessed as extremely high in terms of both scale and urgency. Over three million people required humanitarian assistance of some kind, most of whom required urgent, life-saving or life-sustaining response, while some mainly required livelihood support without being at increased risk to life, health, or safety.

Practical Lessons Learned

a. Chaplains can encourage helping agencies in understanding the "big picture."

Two million people required food assistance. In interacting with faith-based NGOs, some were unable to grasp the logistical challenges of providing transport as well as the appropriateness of their donations. Diana Rothe-Smith, executive director of the National Voluntary Organizations Active in Disaster stated, "A handful of "Help Haiti" food and clothing drives across the country are inspiring cringes among some workers. I would strongly recommend that no donation drives be conducted unless there's an existing organization on the ground, in Haiti, that has asked for the help" Rothe-Smith said. "It does pile up very quickly. Jeff Nene, a spokesman for Convoy of Hope, a Springfield, Mo., agency that feeds 11,000 children a day in Haiti, urges cash donations that allow his group to buy in bulk from large suppliers and retailers. When people give $1, it translates into $7 in the field, he said. If they spend $5 for bottled water, that's nice and it makes them feel good, but probably it costs us more than $5 to send it. If they give us $5, we can get $35 worth of water." That's a sentiment echoed by virtually every aid agency. During Phase II of the operation, a website was established that encouraged direct contact with local Haitian businesses. This was instituted as a result of lessons learned in Afghanistan, where donors endorsed an "Afghan First" Policy. This policy helped ensure that aid money spent on Afghanistan was spent in Afghanistan by using capable local suppliers wherever possible to carry out project work.

Similarly, the "Haiti First" Approach would help stimulate economic growth and stability in the local economy. Chaplains at all levels should make Faith-based NGOs aware of local economic needs and the opportunity to stretch their development dollars and expand their services.

      b. Chaplains can provide a cultural perspective

Both the chaplain and helping organization/group must be aware of potential challenges. Some in Haiti's large Voodoo community feared that Christian relief groups were pursuing ulterior motives. Max Beauvoir, Haiti's chief Voodoo priest, accused foreign Christian groups of —trying to buy souls, and said Haitian Christians —grab scarce resources and receives preferential treatment. He convened a national meeting of Voodooists —unhappy with the attitudes of the Christian community and their foreign guests ... to decide together the future of our country.

The military chaplain can assist the faith-based NGO in understanding the uniqueness of the local population. An awareness of the religious/spiritual climate can give insight on ministry opportunities. Chaplain, LCDR Glenda Jennings-Harrison, USN, serving on the USS Carl Vinson noted, "It was at this moment that I realized that ministering in a setting such as this would require that I first draw upon the discernment of the Holy Spirit, as well as, utilize the life lessons learned from my own experiences. In so doing, this would allow me to approach the art of providing pastoral care in a manner that would take into account the cultural background of a people who shared my ancestry and who understand the spirit world from the eyes of the supernatural.

      a. The chaplain can assist in helping others navigate the challenges of working alongside other

Humanitarian relief actors.

The Haiti earthquake spawned a tremendous humanitarian response.

Moved by awful images of the earthquake, a broad band of religious groups responded. Many chose to act independently and distanced themselves from any interfaith cooperation. Others chose to work together. One unlikely union was the relationship formed between Islamic Relief USA, America's largest Muslim relief organization, and the Church of Jesus Christ of Latter-Day Saints. The two organizations teamed up to provide thousands of pounds of supplies including medical equipment, blankets, quilts, first aid kits, and water filtration bottles. It was an unlikely, but highly effective union.

> a. Chaplains could provide and develop a culture of preparedness prior to a disaster.

Both local and national relief organizations would benefit from a more comprehensive orientation to military logistical and security capabilities. Conferences could be offered to faith-based NGOs to further broaden the understanding of the structure of humanitarian relief operations, the distinctive nature and scope of faith-based NGOs, the role of the military chaplain, and lessons learned.

Ch, Lt Col Randy Marshall

Flight Notes #5

THE CHRISTIAN WARRIOR

Study Guide

Romans 12 concludes with a *prohibition* of *personal*

retribution, yet Paul immediately follows this with a divinely instituted *prescription* for appointed *civil agents* to punish moral evil.

Romans 13:1-4

1. What does "bear the sword" mean in vs 4?

2. What criteria would you use to determine if the use of force is justified?

History of the "Just War Tradition" (see below)
The essence of the "Just War Tradition"
The first part deals with the question of "when"

Proper Declaration

- Just Cause
  The existence of the state or lives of its citizens must be at stake. Self-defense is the only cause for war.
- Lawful Authority
  War should only be undertaken with proper authority
- Just Intent
  The intent of going to war is to promote or secure peace, not merely to obtain revenge, wealth, or personal glory.
- Last Resort
  War should be the final action after negotiations, sanctions, etc…
- Reasonable Hope of Success
  The war must be winnable

The second part of the Just War tradition deals with the question of "what?"

Proper Conduct

- Discrimination
  Warring factions are obligated to discriminate between an

enemy's armed forces and its civilian population. Three groups to be considered are:

--Combatants—All those engaged in the actual promotion of war

--Noncombatants—Chaplains, medical personnel, and civilians

--Neutral—Those not a part of either faction

- Proportionality

The amount and type of force to be utilized in war should be the minimum necessary to end the war and secure peace.

Scripture should be our moral and ethical compass when determining if war is the solution. An understanding of the Just War tradition can be a tremendous help in navigating the difficult issues that believers face in our modern day. The Just War tradition provides a framework to help determine a nation's right to participate in war while defining the participant's proper conduct.

THE JUST-WAR TRADITION
I.   Introduction
The Just-War Tradition provides an ethical and moral framework in understanding the rationale of military engagement. The United States upholds this tradition. Various Department of Defense Directives, codes of conduct, and rules of engagement are built upon the Just-War Tradition. This tradition is at least 2000 years old and is a result of contributions from philosophers, theologians, jurists, statesmen, and warriors.

II.   Historical considerations
The Western tradition of Just War begins with the Roman statesman, Cicero who suggested some simple rules to determine if a war was just. Augustine of Hippo in the 4th century developed the Just-War idea even more. The Roman Emperor Constantine had legalized Christianity in AD 313 and encouraged its growth

by his massive ecclesiastical building projects. Augustine, in contrast to many believers, felt that Christians had a responsibility to civic involvement. This included military involvement. He argued that Christian love at times demanded the use of force to restrain evil. For hundreds of years, the writings of Augustine provided Western civilization with its concept of the morality of war. The chief feature of this understanding was that at times a nation had a right, indeed a duty, to go to war.

In the 13th century, Thomas Aquinas systematized Augustine's position by clearly specifying certain criteria to justify going to war. Aquinas, like Augustine, did not glorify war nor see it as a positive moral good. He made a presumption in favor of peace and held that one who engages in warfare must make a case for such action.

While Augustine and Aquinas had formulated a theory for the just declaration of war, the knights of the Middle Ages provided rules for the proper conduct of war once it had been declared. The tradition of the Just-War thus came to have two major parts, the right to go to war and the right conduct of war. The Latin names given to these two aspects are: the jus ad bellum and the jus in bello.

III.   The Essence of the Just-War Tradition
Jus Ad Bellum—When it is Just—Proper Declaration

Countries are morally and legally bound not to engage in war against one another unless certain criteria are met. These criteria are:

- Just Cause
  The cause should not be as a result of trivial preferences or insults to national pride. Generally, the existence of the state or the lives of its citizens must be at stake. Self-defense is the only just cause for war that is formally recognized in modern international law. It is invoked to protect the lives of its citizens when they are clearly threatened or attacked.
- Lawful Authority
  War should be undertaken only with proper authority

- Just Intent
The intent of going to war is to promote or secure peace, not merely to obtain revenge, wealth, or personal glory.
- Last Resort
War should be the final action. Negotiations, compromises, economic sanctions, appeals for reason, etc should be conducted first.
- Reasonable Hope of Success
A hopeless war is deemed pointless and contrary to common sense and justice.

Jus in Bello- What is just—Proper Conduct
- Discrimination
Warring parties are obligated to discriminate between an enemy's armed forces and its civilian population. There are three groups to be considered in battle:
-- Combatants
All those who are engaged in the actual promotion of war. Direct combatants are the fighters themselves. Indirect combatants are the unarmed helpers of the soldiers in military ways such as transporters of supplies, weapons producers, etc...
-- Noncombatants
Those who are members of the enemy nation that are chaplains, medical personnel and civilians.
-- Neutral people
Those who are not part of either warring party and are not involved in the hostilities.
The killing or wounding of enemy combatants falls under the natural law idea of self-defense. The indirect killing of non-combatants or neutrals is permissible according to principle of double effect. But such killing must be unintentional and unavoidable.
- Proportionality
The amount and type of force to be utilized in war should be the minimum necessary to end war and secure peace.

IV. Conclusion

An understanding of the Just-War tradition can be a tremendous help to those who struggle with the ethical and moral tension of modern-day warfare. This ethical and moral framework is vital in determining a nation's right to participate in war while defining the participant's proper conduct. Therefore, the Just-War tradition should be utilized as a touchstone providing both freedom and limitation.
Ch, Lt Col Randy Marshall

Flight Notes #6

THE BATHSHEBA SYNDROME STUDY GUIDE

Leadership—We are all leaders in some capacity. Leadership demands both

competency and character

Once we lose our character, our influence disintegrates.

We are daily exposed to news of moral and ethical failings among our leaders—political, corporate, military, and religious.

Many believe these failures are a result of hypocrisy, lack of principles, lack of ethical standards, low moral character, etc...

The "Bathsheba Syndrome" suggests that these failures are a result of success and lack of preparedness in dealing with its dilemmas.

Scripture: David went from being a shepherd to the King. He was a righteous man who was devoted to God. With a sudden rise to power and wealth, he became a successful and popular king. The story of David and Bathsheba gives us an insight on how "success" can lead to a spinning vortex of ethical and moral failure. The lessons of King David can be a warning and instruction for us all.

2 Samuel 11

Researchers Dean C. Ludwig and Clinton O. Longenecker coined the phrase "Bathsheba Syndrome while identifying four causes why successful leaders choose personal and professional destructive paths.[2]

Success often allows leaders to become <u>complacent</u> and lose <u>focus</u>.

1. 2 Samuel 11:1-2—"In the spring of the year, at the time when kings normally conduct wars..." "he saw a woman..."
2. Success often leads to <u>privileged access</u> to information, people or objects. 2 Samuel 11:3—"So David sent someone to inquire about the woman..."
3. Success oftentimes provides <u>unrestrained control</u> of organizational resources. 2 Samuel 11:4—"So David sent some messengers to get her..."
4. Success can inflate a leader's belief in his or her personal ability to <u>manipulate outcomes</u>. 2 Samuel 11:5-27—"Send me Uriah the Hittite..."

2 Samuel 12—the rest of the story...Nathan confronting David.
Application: What steps can we take to guard our heart?
Ch, Lt Col Randy Marshall

Acronyms

ABU—Airman Battle Uniform
AETC- Air Education Training Command
AFCENT—Air Force Central Command
AFPC—Air Force Personnel Center
AFR—Air Force Reserve
AFRC—Air Force Reserve Command
AGR—Air Guard Reserve
AOR—Area of Responsibility
ATC—Air Training Command
BDU—Battle Dress Uniform
CAOC—Combined Air and Space Operations Center
CAT-A—Category A, also called "TR," Traditional
Reserve
CAT-B—Category B, also called "IMA," Individual
Mobilization Augmentee
CCII—Chaplain Candidate Intensive Internship
Ch—Chaplain (Air Force Designation)
CMOC—Civil-Military Operations Center
CMSGT—Chief Master Sergeant
COCOM—Combatant Commander
COVID—Coronavirus Disease
DOD—Department of Defense
DFAC—Dining Facility
EDIMGIAFAD—Every Day in Middle Georgia is
Armed Forces Appreciation Day
EDIUSAIAFAD—Every Day in the United States of
America is Armed Forces
Appreciation Day

FARC—Fuerzas Armadas Revolucionarias de Colombia (Revolutionary Armed Forces of Colombia)
GTMO—Guantanamo Bay
GWOT—Global War on Terror
HA/DR—Humanitarian/Disaster Relief
HAST—Humanitarian Assistance Survey Team
JAG—Judge Advocate General
JBSA—Joint Base San Antonio
JOA—Joint Operations Area
MPA—Man-Day
HQ—Headquarters
MRE—Meals Ready to Eat
JTF—Joint Task Force
LTC—Army Lieutenant Colonel
LtCol—Air Force Lieutenant Colonel
MSgt—Air Force Master Sergeant
NGO—Non-Governmental Organization
NORAD—North American Aerospace Defense Command
OODA—Observe, Orient, Decide, Act
PIMA—Puppy in My Armpit
POI—Plan of Instruction
PPC—Public Private Cooperation
PT—Physical Training
RST—Religious Support Team
SFC—Army Sergeant First Class
STX—Simulated Training Exercise
SJFH—Standing Joint Force Headquarters
SME—Subject Matter Expert
SPP—State Partnership Program
SF—Security Forces

TS—Top Secret
USG—United States Government
VOQ—Visiting Officer Quarters
USAID/OFDA—United States Agency for International
Development/Office of United States Foreign Disaster
Assistance
USAFA—United States Air Force Academy
UN—United Nations
USAFRICOM—United States Africa Command
USCENTCOM—United States Central Command
USEUCOM—United States European Command
USINDOPACOM—United States Indo-Pacific
Command
USNORTHCOM—United States Northern Command
USSOUTHCOM—United States Southern Command
YRRP—Yellow Ribbon Program

Notes

The Road to Miami

1. http://www.usachcs.army.mil/chobc
2. http://www.usachcs.army.mil/history/ brief/ chapter_1.htm
3. Ibid
4. http://www.usachcs.army.mil/history/brief
5. https://history.army.mil/html/bookshelves/resmat/desert-storm/index.html
6. Ibid
7. https://www.jbsa.mil/news/news/article/1470075/main-chapel-remains-one-of-jbsa-randolphs-great-jewels/
8. Ibid
9. President George W. Bush, Camp David, 15 September 2001
10. Ibid
11. Lieutenant General James E. Sherrard III, AFRC Commander and CAFR, March 2002
12. https://www.ksat.com/news/local/2021/09/11/she-died-trying-to-help-others-karen-wagners-legacy-endures-20-years-after911/

United States Southern Command

1. https//www.southcom.mil/about/southcom-components-and-units/
2. https://www.southcom.mil/about/leadership/chaplain/
3. https://web.archive.org/web/20200926182247/https:/cgaviation history.org/2003-coast-guard-transferred-to-the-department-of-ho meland-security/
4. https://www.gpo.gov/fdsys/pkg/uscode-2011-title18/pdf/uscode -2011-title18-parti-chap67-sec1385.pdf
5. https//www.jtfgtmo.southcom.mil

6. Romero; New York Times 2008-07-04, p. 3
7. http://www.cnn.com/2008/world/americas/07/03/hostage.drama /index.html
8. https//www.southcom.mil/about
9. https://dbb.defense.gov/portals/35/documents/reports/2012/fy12 -4_public_private_collaboration_in_the_department_of_defense_ 2012-7.pdf
10. https://www.legacy.com/us/obituaries/fresnobee/name/charles-bolin-obituary?id=12080377
11. https://www.southcom.mil/media/special-coverage/panamax-coverage0panamax-2022/
12. Ibid
13. https://pastors.com/8-reasons-church-greatest-force-earth/
14. https:www.af.mil/News/Article-Display/Article/114590/us-southern-command-opens-new-headquarters/
15. https://www.af.mil/news/article-display/article/137626/general-jumper-releases-sight-pictures-covering-character/
16. https://www.loc.gov/everyday-mysteries/zoology/item/why-do-geese-fly-in-a-v/
17. https://www.usmcu.edu/portals/218/ewsonwarreading book1ch1ch.pdf
18. https://www.poetryfoundation.org/poems/157986/high-flight-627d3cfb1e9b7

Al Udeid Air Base

1. https://militarybases.com/overseas/qatar/al-udeid/

Air Force Reserve Command

1. https:www.af.mil/about-us/fact-sheets/display/article/104473/air-force-reserve-command/

2. https://www.nytimes.com/so4/10/26/business/media/a-campaign-for-basf.html
3. https://www.robins.af.mil/News/Artile-Display/Article/378566/ediusaiafad-local-moto-starts-gaining-notice-nationally/
4. https://quotefancy.com quote/1313163/-georg-c-marshall-the-soldier-s-heart-the-soldiers-spirit-the-soldiers-soul/
5. Department of Defense Directive 1300.17, Accommodation of Religious Practices Within the Military Services, and Air Force Instruction 36-2706 Chapter 8, Accommodation of Religious Practices for the Air Force.
6. https://jsc.defense.gov/Portals/99/Documents/MCM2016.pdf?ver=2016-12-08-181411-957
7. AFI 1-2, Air Force Culture, 8 May 2014, para 3.2.4.
8. DODD 1304.19, appointment of Chaplains for the Military Departments, 23 April 2007, para 4.1, 4.2
9. https://www.13wmaz.com/article/news/local/robins-air-force-base/robins-reverses-have-a-blessed-day-is-ok/93-236984078
10. https://www.jstor.org/stable/25072398
11. https://yellowribbon.mil/cms/about-us/

Flight Notes

1. http://www.airpower.maxwell.af.mil/airchronicles/aureview/1978/ju-aug/branham.html
2. http://religionandcocialpolicy.org/finalreport/fullreport060809.pdf3International Review of theRedCross,Volume87 Number860 December 2005
3. http://ksuweb.kennesaw.edu/~uzimmerm/Notes/Ludwig+Longenecker,%20The%20Bathsheba%20Syndrome.pdf and *Naval War College Ethics Symposium* 2013.

Made in the USA
Columbia, SC
05 September 2024

41848651R00141